Teach Like an Ally

Teach Like an Ally

An Educator's Guide to Nurturing LGBTQ+ Students

Flint Del Sol, M.Ed.

JB JOSSEY-BASS™
A Wiley Brand

Copyright © 2025 by John Wiley & Sons, Inc. All rights reserved, including rights for text and data mining and training of artificial intelligence technologies or similar technologies.

Published by John Wiley & Sons, Inc., Hoboken, New Jersey.
Published simultaneously in Canada.

No part of this publication may be reproduced, stored in a retrieval system, or transmitted in any form or by any means, electronic, mechanical, photocopying, recording, scanning, or otherwise, except as permitted under Section 107 or 108 of the 1976 United States Copyright Act, without either the prior written permission of the Publisher, or authorization through payment of the appropriate per-copy fee to the Copyright Clearance Center, Inc., 222 Rosewood Drive, Danvers, MA 01923, (978) 750-8400, fax (978) 750-4470, or on the web at www.copyright.com. Requests to the Publisher for permission should be addressed to the Permissions Department, John Wiley & Sons, Inc., 111 River Street, Hoboken, NJ 07030, (201) 748-6011, fax (201) 748-6008, or online at http://www.wiley.com/go/permission.

The manufacturer's authorized representative according to the EU General Product Safety Regulation is Wiley-VCH GmbH, Boschstr. 12, 69469 Weinheim, Germany, e-mail: Product_Safety@wiley.com.

Trademarks: Wiley and the Wiley logo are trademarks or registered trademarks of John Wiley & Sons, Inc. and/or its affiliates in the United States and other countries and may not be used without written permission. All other trademarks are the property of their respective owners. John Wiley & Sons, Inc. is not associated with any product or vendor mentioned in this book.

Limit of Liability/Disclaimer of Warranty: While the publisher and author have used their best efforts in preparing this book, they make no representations or warranties with respect to the accuracy or completeness of the contents of this book and specifically disclaim any implied warranties of merchantability or fitness for a particular purpose. No warranty may be created or extended by sales representatives or written sales materials. The advice and strategies contained herein may not be suitable for your situation. You should consult with a professional where appropriate. Further, readers should be aware that websites listed in this work may have changed or disappeared between when this work was written and when it is read. Neither the publisher nor authors shall be liable for any loss of profit or any other commercial damages, including but not limited to special, incidental, consequential, or other damages.

For general information on our other products and services or for technical support, please contact our Customer Care Department within the United States at (800) 762-2974, outside the United States at (317) 572-3993 or fax (317) 572-4002.

Wiley also publishes its books in a variety of electronic formats. Some content that appears in print may not be available in electronic formats. For more information about Wiley products, visit our web site at www.wiley.com.

Library of Congress Cataloging-in-Publication Data:

Names: Sol, Flint Del, author.
Title: Teach like an ally : an educator's guide to nurturing LGBTQ+ students / Flint Del Sol.
Description: [San Francisco] : Jossey-Bass, [2025] | Includes bibliographical references and index.
Identifiers: LCCN 2025007069 (print) | LCCN 2025007070 (ebook) | ISBN 9781394291571 (paperback) | ISBN 9781394291595 (adobe pdf) | ISBN 9781394291588 (epub)
Subjects: LCSH: Sexual minority students. | Classroom environment. | Allyship. | Teachers—Training of.
Classification: LCC LC2574 .S65 2025 (print) | LCC LC2574 (ebook) | DDC 371.826/6—dc23/eng/20250326
LC record available at https://lccn.loc.gov/2025007069
LC ebook record available at https://lccn.loc.gov/2025007070

Cover Design: Wiley
Cover Image: © nathapolHPS/Shutterstock
Author Photo by Ali Vesey Photography

SKY10112958_060725

For Reggie

Table of Contents

	Foreword	xi
	Introduction	xiii
	A Final Revision	xiii
	The Master's House	xvii
	The Designated Queer	xix
	The Promise We Make to Ourselves	xxii
	Supplementary Materials	xxv
PART I	**Why Any of This Matters**	**1**
CHAPTER 1	**A Brief and Recent History of the Author**	**3**
	Once a Teacher…	3
	The Letters After Our Names	6
	Who Is Worth Listening To	8
CHAPTER 2	**A Brief and Recent History of LGBTQ+ Issues in the Classroom**	**11**
	Finding the Beginning	11
	Why Is It Always Kids?	12

	Here the Whole Time	15
	A Different Kind of Climate Change	18
	As the Water Begins to Warm	19
	The Boiling Point	21
	The Bright Side	24
CHAPTER 3	**A Brief and Not-So-Recent History of LGBTQ+ Teaching**	**29**
	Life in a Fishbowl	29
	In the Beginning	31
	And the Accusations Roll In	34
	The Pie Heard 'Round the World	37
	My Name Is Harvey Milk, and I'm Here to Recruit You	38
	Queer Teachers Today	40
CHAPTER 4	**Let's Talk Numbers**	**47**
	Finding the Numbers	47
	The Kids Are All Gay	48
	Checking the Facts Against the Feelings	49
	The Seeds and the Soil	52
	The Data Behind the Schoolhouse Door	54
	But…But…the Children!	56
PART II	**Get Your Mind Right**	**61**
CHAPTER 5	**But What Can I Do on Monday?**	**63**
CHAPTER 6	**Taking Inventory**	**67**
	If You're Asking, You Know	67
	What Are You Already Doing?	68

	The Rainbow-Washed Classroom	75
	Grant Me the Grace to Accept the Things I Cannot Change	79
CHAPTER 7	**The Mental Environment**	**83**
	The Space Within the Space	83
	On the Way in the Door	84
	Shifting Classroom Language	86
	Swerving Around the Power Struggle	89
	Let's Take a Walk	93
PART III	**Inside the Classroom**	**97**
CHAPTER 8	**Classroom Policies**	**99**
	WTF Is a Safe Space?	99
	For Safety or Control?	105
	Setting Expectations and Evaluating Policies	107
CHAPTER 9	**The Physical Environment**	**117**
	Check the Space	117
	Flags and Signage	120
	Books and Libraries	124
	What Else Can I Do?	128
CHAPTER 10	**Units and Lessons**	**131**
	Willing to Try	131
	Creativity and Connection	133
	Avoiding Pitfalls	135
	Running an Effective Discussion	137
	Bridging the Confidence Gap	139
	Starting Points (by Subject)	143
	Is It Worth It?	149

PART IV	**Beyond the Classroom**	**153**
CHAPTER 11	**Communicating with Families**	**155**
	A Letter to the Mother Who Called Me a Groomer	155
	We Are Not Enemies	157
	Considerations for Queer Families	162
	Frequent Parent Questions and Concerns	164
	Resources and Recommendations	168
CHAPTER 12	**Make Your Principal Read This Chapter**	**171**
	Are You in the Arena Too?	171
	Leading a Proactive vs. Reactive Campus	174
	Queer Staff Protection and Management	179
CHAPTER 13	**School Board Meetings 101**	**183**
	Why We Hate Robert's Rules	185
	It's Parks and Rec, But Nothing Is Funny	188
	Know the Rules, Know the Game	189
CHAPTER 14	**LGBTFAQs**	**197**
	Quick Tips for GSAs	197
	Logistical Nightmares	201
	Annoying Questions	204
	Acknowledgments	**209**
	Index	**211**

Foreword

Dear Reader,

I, maybe not unlike yourself, am at the start of this book wondering how I got here. I'm V Spehar, creator of Under The Desk News, which started as an early pandemic-era TikTok channel and has continued for many years since as "a safe space for news." Technically, I met Flint through the power of social media. Spiritually, Flint was sent to me as a collaborator, friend, sometimes therapist, picker upper, and reminder that "we can." We can live our most authentic lives, we can grow and change in many ways, we can love others and ourselves...and we can decide to step away from where we are told we are needed to trust the universe to deliver us to a place where we can do the most good. Flint spent many years in the classroom with a group of 100 or so very lucky students per year. Now, he has removed the physical walls and limitations of what we think of as "school" and given us this place, this book, and the community that will spring up out of it – to learn.

I am also very humbled by the idea that Flint Del Sol, a human with compassion as deep as the ocean and a call to justice as strong as the bat signal would ask me to say a few words to warm up the crowd. Flint doesn't need anyone to warm up a crowd, a room, or a book in this case for them. The warmth and optimism they bring to this work serves as not just the proverbial light at the end of the tunnel, but Flint is the guy in the tunnel with an industrial flashlight, headlamps for us all, and a snack or two. He doesn't expect us to find our way in the darkness of unknowing to the light but rather understands many of us need someone to hold our hand through the tunnel.

You may feel nervous or maybe even a little scared or alone getting into this work. You're not alone. Flint packed our day bags and is a trusted guide. Thousands of us are on this journey of being a better ally and teacher together. Everything you need to be a better ally and build a safer space for LGBTQ+ youth you'll find in the pages to follow. You're on your way to being someone's "emotional support teacher"!

When Flint told me he was writing a book, I asked, "Is this book gonna make me cry?" He laughed in a knowing way and said, "Probably!"

I cry a lot, and I cried a lot reading the early editions of this as an adult LGBTQ+ person who wished so much that the solutions provided in this book had been available when I was growing up. That's the rub: we become the adult we needed when we were a kid. We write the solutions to problems no one could solve for us. There's a certain kind of grief in that, and a certain kind of beauty.

That brings me to how to read and use this book.

Skip around. Nothing like this has ever existed in this way before. Your natural inclination will be to *rush* through it to see how it ends and what's inside – do it! Or flash read it, taking a bite out of every chocolate in the box so you know what flavors are where and which are your favorites. Go back and read it again, get a pen out, write in the margins – this is *your* book. Your guide. Dog ear pages, break the spine, spill coffee on it. *Use this book.*

You may have purchased it hoping once you had read it, you'd have something to give someone else. But Flint wrote it hoping to give something to you. Accept the gift. Enjoy the read. You can trust Flint to get you through this tunnel.

V Spehar

Introduction

> "For the master's tools will never dismantle the master's house. They may allow us temporarily to beat him at his own game, but they will never enable us to bring about genuine change."
>
> Audre Lorde

A Final Revision

It is 5:30 p.m. Pacific Standard time on November 6, 2024. I have been researching and writing this book since April, and the manuscript is now due in just nine days. This means you are, right now, reading first what I have written last. Funnily enough, this is how I always tell my students to write, because, as I would say, *you don't know what your point is really going to turn out to be until you've finished*. For even the most seasoned writers (and teachers), though we often start with a plan, we can't guarantee that we'll stick to it. There's just no way to know what will happen in the middle.

For example, less than 24 hours ago, Donald Trump was elected to his second presidential term, by what right now looks like both the popular and the electoral vote. By the time anyone reads this, I'm sure the shock will have worn off, but for right now, it is radiating in a red hum through the ends of my fingertips. I can also feel the pressure of my internal editor, begging me:

Don't get political. *Please.*

For as long as I have been a teacher, I have heard my most well-meaning colleagues, friends, and administrators beg the same. To *get political* has become an educational death knell. *Politics don't belong in the classroom*, I would hear. *It's not worth it. Just don't bother.*

But there is no such place as an apolitical classroom. Every corner of it has been litigated and debated and legislated, from the content of the textbooks to the American flag screwed to the wall. Governing bodies vote on the acceptable length of a teen girl's skirt, football coaches lead teams in pre-game prayer, and we have asked every school-age child to stand for a recitation of the Pledge of Allegiance since the late 1800s.

No matter how you feel about any of it, the classroom is a political place. Full stop.

So, if that's true, why do I feel that I've been uniquely singled out here? Why am I, a teacher who went more than a decade without indicating a candidate or party preference in front of his students, accused so frequently of *getting political*?

Because I'm trans.

Flint, the name you see on the cover of this book, was not the name my mother gifted to me when I was born. And although it took almost 30 years, when I started to understand that the restless, unsettled, sideways feeling living in my chest had a name, I acted on it. I cut my hair. I changed my name. I started taking hormones. And almost immediately, that restless, unsettled, sideways feeling *evaporated*. I looked in the mirror and recognized myself for the first time. I felt at home in a body that always felt like it was on loan. I realized both that I was finally happy and that real happiness had been a stranger to me for the entirety of my life.

While I was experiencing this – while I was learning and growing into who I was – I was also teaching eleventh- and twelfth-grade English at a public high school.

People like me – trans people, gay people, or really anyone within the alphabet soup acronym that I always lose track of – are made political against our will. There is no "opt out" option when you make the choice to live authentically, even when some members of our community promise to abandon the others in the name of a more frictionless assimilation. No one came by to check our individual party registrations when politicians chose to run more than $65 million in anti-trans ads from August through October in 2024.[i] What made us political was not what we believed or who we supported, but who we *were*.

The same is true for educators, especially those of us who choose to work in public schools, regardless of our gender or sexual orientation. Teachers and classrooms will remain political as long as decisions about them are made by politicians, for better or for worse. And we have a duty to care for and educate the children entrusted to us, no matter where they were born, if and how they worship, or what their family looks like. That choice is political too.

So where did this book start, and where did it end?

When I first set out, I wanted to write a guide that you could slap into the hands of any educator in the country. I wanted everyone to be able to find *something* they could implement immediately, that they could feel confident trying, even if they didn't understand everything about the LGBTQ+ community. I wanted easy entry-level options to help break the seal on a barrier of fear that some teachers wouldn't even know was there. I wanted even just one queer kid to feel an iota safer in just one classroom. And though I'm positive I've done that (and done it well), my purpose has since gotten a little larger.

---

[i] Goldmacher, Shane. "Trump and Republicans Bet Big on Anti-Trans Ads across the Country." *The New York Times*, October 8, 2024. https://www.nytimes.com/2024/10/08/us/politics/trump-republican-transgender-ads.html.

Because I have this creeping feeling right now that as hard as it is to be an effective and caring teacher for LGBTQ+ students, it's about to get even harder. It's a feeling that's telling me Florida's "Don't Say Gay" will soon become national policy, that book bans are just at their infancy, and that the growing numbers of LGBTQ+ youth mental health disparities are about to balloon. I hope I'm wrong, but I don't think I am.

That is why I'm glad this book took a turn as I was writing it.

Because while many books focus exclusively on queer-centered interventions (think Gay–Straight Alliances, nondiscrimination policies, rainbow flags, schoolwide Pride events), that's not what's going to happen here. Because while all those clubs, policies, and initiatives are helpful, they can also be taken away. Every school in the country is just one school board meeting away from walking away with straight bupkis for their LGBTQ+ population. And then what will we do?

We know that it's possible, because it's already happening. There are classrooms across the nation where teachers are contractually forbidden from using a nickname for a student unless their parents expressly consent or where there exists not a single book featuring a character or storyline that is not expressly heterosexual. All, of course, in the name of avoiding *politics*.

Most of this book is for those classrooms, both for today and into the uncertain future.

Because while, on its surface, *Teaching Like an Ally* might sound like sticking a pronoun pin on your blazer and a rainbow flag in your pencil cup, the work is much deeper. Truly committing to educational allyship means standing as the lone voice in a room filled to the brim with bigotry. It means listening to students and colleagues who might be too angry and tired to be polite. And perhaps hardest, it means reflecting on your teaching practice with potentially painful honesty.

There is no price for entry. It doesn't matter who you've voted for (or if you've ever voted at all), where you live, or how you identify.

In fact, you don't have to be a teacher at all. The only requirement for moving on from here is a commitment to trying your best for every LGBTQ+ child who will have to navigate this world without very much help.

So, if you're ready, let's get started.

The Master's House

Public education isn't a huge fan of variety and difference. In fact, it is built on the assumption that children of an infinite number of backgrounds, experiences, and needs have the same chance to thrive under the same set of extremely narrow circumstances. For seven hours a day, we ask our students to work around our schedule, waking up before their internal clocks are ready, transitioning between radically different physical and social spaces, and taking in an astounding amount of new information while they navigate alarming and unfamiliar emotional waters. All the while, their homes, their brains, their bodies, their resources, and their generational histories are all different. We're sticking every seed in the same air-conditioned fluorescently lit garden box and hoping for the best.

Change is finding its way into schools, but it's historically slow-moving. There are an overwhelming number of large systemic issues we need to address if we want to truly be allies to every kind of student, but that doesn't mean there's nothing we can do on our own right now. Every person who works inside a school can effect change and brighten the reality of the children who move through the building each day. No one educator or principal or parent is going to dismantle the system in one blow, but there is quite a bit within our control, and we do have the individual power to earn ground in a battle of inches that will likely continue long after we're gone.

If we decide we're committed to trying, there's some learning and unlearning that has to happen first. Because to figure out how to be flexible, adaptive, affirming, and welcoming for LGBTQ+ students, we have to understand that we've been repeatedly and consistently conditioned to be rigid, stubborn, and exclusionary.

And it's mostly not our fault (*I promise*).

Even if we don't want to see it, there's a cynical and corrosive way of thinking and being that gradually creeps in within education, and it's the result of being confronted repeatedly by unrealistic and sky-high expectations paired with infuriating and impossible circumstances.

I think about my time as a student teacher, when I first had to take the theoretical pedagogical values I'd spent years building up for myself and test them against the day-to-day realities of a high school classroom.

The ideology of positivity and empathy is easy, but the practice is much harder, if not impossible. This is why many teachers pivot to angry doodling and group texting when they sit through mandatory professional developments led by bouncy facilitators who have never seen the inside of a classroom. We're asked constantly to add to our plates, take on ever-draining emotional labor, and provide rigorous cutting-edge instruction for students who seem to be falling further and further behind.

All of that would be hard enough on its own, but it's continuously compounded by the looming specter of public opinion. Schools are lightning rods for local community (and sometimes even national) criticism, and nothing makes a hard job harder like anonymous Facebook feedback.

All of this is swirling inside of us when we're asked to take another look at the way we run our classrooms, or our schools as a whole. We want answers that fit seamlessly into what we are already doing, answers that align with the curriculum map we made in July, answers that will not take more than the 1 minutes between classes to implement. We're willing to shift our paradigms, but not if we have to use the clutch.

And this is the insidious danger of promising quick fixes: there aren't any.

Really and truly nurturing LGBTQ+ students is not a matter of putting our pronouns in our email signatures and calling it a day. It will mean changing the way we approach our students as individuals and rethinking the educational models that have kept them shut out and pushed to the edge for decades.

First, we will never know everything about a student because we know *something* about them. A kid isn't just a summary of their demographic information, and there are no quick and easy steps to fostering a patient, loving, and radically healing school and classroom culture. In this book, there won't be shortcuts to understanding, because being queer is only ever a small part of someone's story. Your queer kids are also foster kids; they're Muslim, they're Black, they're food insecure, they're neurodivergent, they're immigrants. Erase the idea that these are separate boxes.

Despite the complicated nature of identity, it's also true that the systems most likely to hurt queer students are the same ones that hurt all students, and to that end, addressing them is in everyone's best interest. From rigid policies and curriculum to a critical lack of access to support staff and counselors, there's a lot that needs our attention.

And remember there are plenty of hurtful systems that govern our lives, but let's not lay down on the hot cement with our arms by our sides and disintegrate in powerlessness.

Factory farms don't keep us from planting gardens. Global hunger doesn't keep us from starting community food banks. An imperfect education system shouldn't keep us from finding ways to make life a smidgeon less devastating for the queer students we see every day.

The Designated Queer

Within queer circles, there's a phrase you'll hear over and over when people are up to discussing their time served in secondary education:

"Emotional Support English Teacher."

You don't have to be an English teacher to be an Emotional Support English Teacher. From experience, this person is the one adult who cares loudly enough to lower the defenses erected throughout a lifetime of growing up queer. If they aren't in the English building, they're often in the ceramics studio, the art room, or the activities office. There is one outstanding consensus: their subject is within the arts and humanities, they're often women, and they are usually queer.

As a proud Emotional Support English Teacher, it took me a long time to have anything other than good feelings about it. I loved knowing that my LGBTQ+ students sought comfort in my council and felt safe in my classroom. It was a delight to consider that of all the adults they knew, I was the one they considered a soft place to land in an often-cruel environment. It wasn't until I was near the end of my tenure, a full decade later, when I finally picked my head up and looked around to wonder: "Wait, where the hell is everyone else?"

> **Triggering Language Warning**
>
> *The following story uses potentially triggering anti-LGBTQ+ language. Proceed with caution!*
>
> One afternoon, when I was deep into my emotional support English teacher era, a student I'd never seen before knocked on my classroom door during lunch. She was a friend of a student of mine, who had been referred my way when she wasn't sure who to talk to. Like many teenagers who need help but don't know how to ask, it took a bit of coaxing and an extended uncomfortable silence for her to open up. When she did, she told me what was on her mind.
>
> She was gay, she said, and she'd known long before high school, and over the last few months she had been agonizing over

how to tell her parents. They weren't hateful people, she told me, but she had spent years trying to find evidence that they would support her, and she kept coming up short. She listened in on her brother playing video games online with his friends, where he would often call opponents "fags" without intervention from her family. She listened to her father nudge her siblings during moments of vulnerability, telling them "not to be so queer." She watched him fast-forward through same-sex kissing scenes in movies, sticking his tongue out in discomfort. She went to baby and bridal showers with her mother, who never missed an opportunity to tell her how excited she was for her daughter to one day be a happy wife and mother.

These incidents might feel small, but they added up to a whole that she couldn't ignore. She didn't have clear evidence that they would reject her, but she also didn't have any that they wouldn't.

There is a common misconception that a queer person's signs of safety are overt and obvious and that our moments of pain are glaring and clear, but our picture of discomfort is usually a death by a thousand cuts. It's the consistent messaging we can't help but hear: our identity is not the default, and we will be unwelcomed and ostracized if we're honest about who we are.

This is why caring is everyone's business.

The sun is setting on the time of the emotional support English teacher. Only when a whole host of adults in every corner of a school campus come together to actively create intentional safe and welcoming spaces for queer students will they feel that their school belongs to them too. Inaction and indifference are not neutral; there is no "staying out of it." This is going to take all of us.

The Promise We Make to Ourselves

Teachers are supposed to be lifelong learners – that's our whole thing. We want to lean into curiosity; that's where we thrive, that's what we want to inspire in our students. Whenever I mentored a new teacher, the first advice I passed along to them was that if they loved their content area more than they loved learning and understanding the needs of young adults, they might be in the wrong profession. What matters more than subject competence is always going to be the interest in and stamina for growth, for them and for us.

Education is a dynamic field that always has something new to offer us, and it's our choice what to do with it when we're confronted by change that makes us uncomfortable. Ultimately, when we stagnate, our craft suffers. So many of us work through careers that started from a place of genuine optimism and empathy to find that one day we stop remembering what it was like to be young, what it was like to be doubted in our experience of our lives and in our bodies, what it was like to be ignored and unheard. All I'm asking as you make your way through any part of this book is to try to access that person again: the one who knew that you might not have all the answers.

As you explore what I have to offer you here, don't be surprised when something challenges you, even if you consider yourself a staunch ally, because that's what *Teach Like an Ally* means. Allyship isn't a badge; it isn't a reward you earn after 40 hours of professional development and a multiple-choice "check for understanding." It's a living, growing promise to believe that you always have more to learn, even within communities of which you are part.

As a trans person who has experienced his fair share of horrifying human behavior, I'm still a firm believer that the most heartbreaking attitudes often come from our "allies" when it becomes obvious that support is conditional, to be revoked when their comfort is challenged. *I shouldn't have to change,* we often hear. *You shouldn't criticize those of us who do so much for you.*

Being open to criticism and self-reflection is exactly what makes someone an ally.

There's no finish line here.

Holding support hostage in the need for the protection of your own comfort isn't dismantling the master's house; it's adding another layer of cement to the foundation.

So, turn these pages with an open mind and the assumption that something will eventually rub you the wrong way. Sit in the feeling, talk yourself through why it might be coming up for you, and hold yourself with the same compassion you would extend to any of the students in your care. Teachers, education support professionals, counselors, administrators, parents, families: anyone who has a hand in the growth and support of our students in schools will find resources and welcome here. Now, let's take the next step of this journey together – we're going to need each other.

Supplementary Materials

Visit www.delsolimpact.com/teach-like-an-ally to access even more resources, such as a sample schoolwide "transition plan," my "getting to know you" student survey, a students' rights poster pack, an LGBTQ+ ally classroom checklist, and more!

Notes from the Queer Teacher Survival Guide

Welcome to the Queer Teacher Survival Guide!

Reading this book as a queer teacher is going to hit different, so in every chapter (sometimes more than once), you will see a little box like this that will offer a perspective acknowledging that. Not every queer experience in a school is the same, but we are connected by a largely universal feeling of isolation and frequent tokenization. We are rarely seen in discussions about campus climate, and our lives and identities are often discussed as if we aren't in the room. We're invited to sit on panels, called on to supervise GSAs,[i] and asked to access our experiences to help our cisgender and straight colleagues and community learn and grow, but we are also held to an impossible standard: live authentically as an example for the students who look up to us, but don't talk openly about our lives. Be proud of our differences, but don't look or talk or act differently. We watch our colleagues down through kindergarten stage engagement announcements and gender reveals in the classroom, but we're asked to keep photos of our families off our desks and remove rainbow stickers from our laptops. We haven't lived every queer identity that we see reflected in our students, and so we are still allies, but our role in this work is very different. It's deeply personal for us. So, as you read, remember to take moments to find compassion and space for yourself – you are waking up every day and showing up as the adult you needed to see. That's enough.

And if you aren't part of this community, these boxed sections are still for you. As you navigate this book, take the time to consider the weight your queer colleagues are carrying with them. Even if you see your campus as a safe and equitable space for students, how does that carry through (or not) to the staff? What space is being made for them? It is very likely that there are adults on your campus – supervisors, nurses, counselors, custodians, teachers, administrators, nutrition staff, paraeducators – "out" or not, who are having a much different experience than you realize. Remember them too.

---

[i] A GSA is a campus student group whose letters used to stand for "Gay-Straight Alliance," but that has shifted largely to "Gender and Sexuality Alliance." GSAs go by many names across the country, and they may use a different title entirely, such as "Rainbow Alliance" or "Queer Student Alliance."

LGBTQ+ 101: Terminology Guide

How to Use This Guide

Nothing stresses out allies quite like queer terminology.

There's a pervasive fear that using the wrong word for someone's identity or experience is akin to throwing us from a moving train into an active forest fire, but honestly, it doesn't have to be that serious. The reason why language is such a pain point for all of us (that is, for both the LGBTQ+ community and our allies) is that it's the most likely and visible interaction that we will experience between our values. For a trans person like me, I don't have to find out how strangers feel about my community until they have a reason to talk about us, and the words they use will give me a quick assessment of how much knowledge and experience they're bringing to the table. For allies, searching for the "right" word can feel impossible without a glossary of terms queued up and ready to go, and the chances of failure keep climbing higher and higher the longer that glossary becomes.

But language isn't a trap; it's the structure for how we think about and relate to our own experiences and the experiences of other people, and being "right" 100% of the time is much less important than being curious and kind. The terms the LGBTQ+ community uses to talk about ourselves are constantly changing, because we keep learning more and more about the specifics and intricacies of our wholly unique lives. Yes, it was easier to learn how to talk about us when the only other option was "gay," but just like a houseplant stuck in too small a pot, we were only able to grow to the edge of our constructed limits. As language evolves, so do we. It's a unique kind of blessing to get to be here to see it happen.

It's important also to remember that queer identity is more of a union than a country club. Because so many of us have lived in isolation and resentment as part of the "out" group within the general population, we have this internal pull to want to control the boundaries of who can get in with us when we're finally on the "inside." For these definitions, I tend to err on the side of inclusivity, with a huge asterisk over the whole thing that says "These definitions are a starting point to learn how we talk about ourselves right now, but change is nature, the world continues to grow and shift, and I reserve the right to be completely wrong later."

So how should you approach these terms in the meantime?

Consider that all of us are very much like cats and that a term or a label is an inviting cardboard box. Cats often choose to put themselves into boxes but don't usually like being stuck inside them against their will, even when it seems like they will fit. It's always best to ask someone what words they like to use for themselves and to trust them when they tell you, even if it goes against your current understanding. We're the experts in ourselves, and we all deserve the chance to figure it out in our own time.

AFAB/AMAB (pronounced "ayy-fab"/"ayy-mab")

Acronyms for "assigned female at birth" and "assigned male at birth." These are terms often used in transgender circles to discuss our unique experiences related to the gender we were assigned at birth but aren't generally common or preferred when we hear from allies.

"She says she wants to be more inclusive to trans people in her study, but she's still only talking to AFABs, which isn't ideal or inclusive."

Ally

Can be used as a noun or a verb, for both a person who prioritizes and advocates on behalf of a marginalized community, and the action of following through on that advocacy in the world. Allyship isn't a badge you earn once, never to be looked at again, but a consistent attitude that asks us to examine and re-examine how we show up for each other.

"I want to be an ally for the LGBTQ+ community, so I bought five copies of this book the day it hit the shelves."

Asexual/Aromantic
Identities rooted in the lack of sexual or romantic attraction (or both), commonly shortened to "ace."

"Why is there an asexual flag on the Pride parade float? Because ace people are queer too!"

Bisexual
A sexual identity where an individual has the capacity to be attracted to more than one gender. There's a common misconception that "bi" must mean two, as in "only attracted to men and women," but historically "bi" has meant attraction to both "same" and "other" genders.

"My roommate has only ever been with one partner, but she is still very much bisexual."

Deadname
The name a transgender person was given at birth but no longer uses in their own life. It can also be used as a verb, as in "deadnaming," or the action of using a trans person's former name. It is generally considered to be not only rude, but often dangerous, to ask for or use a trans person's deadname.

"I updated my name on my driver's license three years ago, but my deadname still shows up on my phone bill no matter what I do."

Gay
A common catchall sexual identity for someone who is attracted to people of their same gender. Over time, this term has become more flexible and inclusive and does not just refer to gay men or people who are solely same-sex attracted.

"When I'm talking to someone new, I want to explain that I am a genderqueer pansexual, but for the sake of simplicity I usually just say I'm gay."

Gender

Separate from sex, which is determined often by biological factors such as chromosomes, hormones, and reproductive anatomy, gender is constructed socially. All people have a gender identity, which we represent in our behaviors, activities, and how we relate to one another.

"He told me that I can't like that show, paint my nails, or wear these clothes because I'm a boy, but I get to decide how to express and live in my gender."

Gender/Sex Assigned at Birth

Though sex and gender are different, most of us are assigned a gender (as well as a sex) at birth. Most Western medical protocols ask for healthcare professionals to determine a baby's gender and mark it on their birth certificate, though more states in the United States are beginning to offer "X" as an option to decline this process, instead of just "M" or "F."

"They were born intersex, but the doctor still recorded their gender assigned at birth as female."

Gender Creative

Describes someone who is questioning and/or "playing fast and loose" with the societally imposed boundaries of gender, though they may not identify as explicitly transgender. It is most used when talking about children who show an early interest in living outside of gendered expectations.

"Gender creative kids are going to save the world. My neighbor's kid just shrugged and went back to playing when someone asked if they were a boy or a girl. I love that energy."

Genderfluid

A gender identity that describes the experience of movement between genders without a consistent fixed point. A genderfluid person may move between feeling like a man, a woman, neither, both, or all.

"They're genderfluid, so they told me that they want to use 'they/them' today even though the last time I saw them, they preferred 'she/her'."

Gender Nonconforming

Someone who is gender nonconforming (sometimes also called GNC) doesn't adhere to the expectations or norms of their gender assigned at birth. It's not just trans people who are commonly gender nonconforming – anyone can push the boundaries of what is expected of them within their gender.

"Did you know the white stripe that you see in a lot of Pride flags is usually there to recognize nonbinary and gender nonconforming experiences in our communities? Very cool."

GSA/QSA

When I was a student in school, the GSA was an extracurricular student club where the letters stood for "Gay–Straight Alliance." Since then, they've rebranded to the "Gender and Sexuality Alliance" for the purposes of inclusivity. The other names you'll see for student clubs like this might also be the "Rainbow Alliance" or "Queer Student Alliance."

"Every time I see a student speaking at a school board meeting, I always find out after that they're the president of their school's GSA. This generation is doing amazing work."

GSM

An umbrella term meaning "gender and sexual minorities" commonly found in medical or legal writing and documentation. While it is inclusive, it is not often used by people within the community to describe their identities or experiences.

"Even though there are a ton of letters in LGBTQ+, I still prefer it to GSM when talking about our lives, laws, and healthcare."

Heteronormativity

The expectation that everyone is heterosexual and values and prioritizes heterosexual lives and experiences above all others. The assumption baked into heteronormativity is that to be "straight" is the natural, biological default of human existence, which it is not.

"Even though she expressed attraction to girls when she was younger, shaved her head, replaced her entire wardrobe with flannel, and listens exclusively to Chappell Roan, K. D. Lang, and Hayley Kiyoko, her grandma still asks her when she's going to find the 'right man.' Thanks, heteronormativity."

Intersex

Someone who is intersex has biological traits, such as chromosomes, hormones, or reproductive anatomy, that fall between the anticipated medical determinations of binary sex (that is, male or female). Though about 1 out of every 100 people are born intersex, they are often assigned a binary sex at birth and, though the practice is falling out of fashion, frequently subjected to natal "corrective" surgery.

"Did you know that the number of intersex people in the United States is almost exactly equal to the number of redheads?"

Lesbian

At its most technical, this is a term used to describe women who experience attraction solely to other women, though practically and historically, it can be much broader. There are many people identifying as lesbians who include gender nonconforming, nonbinary, or other non-cisgender male identities within the scope of the term.

"Even though lesbian activism has always been the foundation of the queer community, there are currently only 32 lesbian bars operating in the United States."

Nonbinary

Someone whose gender identity falls outside of the binary of either "man" or "woman." Nonbinary is not a third gender but rather a large umbrella term to describe a continuum of experiences that do not adhere to binary gender expectations. Sometimes abbreviated to "nb" or "enby."

"My nonbinary teacher doesn't use Ms or Mr but asked us to put "Mx" in front of their name, pronounced like 'mix'."

Neuroqueer

Used to describe the unique intersection of experiences lived by individuals who are both neurodivergent and queer, as those of us in one of these communities is more likely to be part of the other. Neurodivergence can include, but is not limited to, attention-deficit/hyperactivity disorder (ADHD), autism, post-traumatic stress disorder (PTSD), Tourette's, obsessive–compulsive disorder (OCD), and dyslexia.

"I could say that I am an autistic and ADHD trans man, but it's faster to say that I'm neuroqueer."

Pansexual

Similar to bisexual, someone who is pansexual has the capacity to experience attraction to both same and different genders, though a distinction is important to many people within this community. Whereas "bi" suggests that someone may be limited in the number of genders to which they experience attraction (though this is not always true), "pan" suggests that all genders are on the table.

"I've had the difference between bisexual and pansexual explained to me 10 times and I still feel like I'm missing something, so I picked the one that I think has the prettier flag."

Passing

To be "passing" as a queer person means that it is likely challenging for a straight or cisgender stranger to determine that they are queer. For trans people, this means that most people would assume that their presented gender is also the gender they were assigned at birth. For sexual identities, this means that most people would assume they are heterosexual. "Passing" is not always a choice and is sometimes unwanted. Many queer people feel that they have to work to "pass" to guarantee their safety in public.

"I started taking testosterone almost a year ago, and I only started passing recently when my voice dropped."

Pronouns

Despite recent bad press and misinformation, pronouns have always been part of communication in English. These are the shortened words that replace nouns, and the best way to know which pronouns someone would like to use for themselves is to ask. The most common pronouns for people are she/her, he/him, and they/them, but there are less common options like xi/xir, or blended pronouns (where someone is open to more than one choice), such as she/they.

"When you tell me that you 'don't have' pronouns, I know immediately that you have no idea what pronouns are."

Queer

A reclaimed umbrella term used to describe LGBTQ+ people and their experiences. Though once used as a slur, it is much more common to see this designation used in academic, medical, and casual circumstances than it once was. For allies especially, it is important to remember that queer is an adjective and not a noun, so someone can be a queer person but should not be called "a queer." Many people also use this term to describe their sexual orientation in looser terms than any other options provide.

"We're here, we're queer, get used to it!"

Sexuality/Sexual Identity/Sexual Orientation

Separate from gender identity, which is exclusively an internal sense of gender, sexual identity is a determination of sexual or romantic attraction to other people. A person could have the potential to be attracted to their same gender, people of different genders, or no one at all.

"Every time I see a question on a form that asks me my sexual orientation, I don't know if I should mark 'queer,' 'gay,' or 'lesbian,' so I just circle all of them and hope for the best."

SOGI

An acronym for "sexual orientation and gender identity," used primarily in data collection spaces, especially when discussing the kinds of questions that should be asked, to whom they should be asked, and what should be done with the data afterward.

"We know that asking SOGI questions in student surveys is beneficial for our equity work, but we have to also consider the ways we can keep that data safe."

Transfem/transmasc

These are terms used to describe the experiences of trans people who lean or present more on the "feminine" side if they are AMAB, or on the "masculine" side if they are AFAB. Someone who identifies as transfem or transmasc may also consider themselves a trans woman or a trans man, or they may not, instead preferring to identify as nonbinary or another adjacent term.

"I have never walked into a coffee shop that didn't have the most handsome transmasc in the world working behind the espresso machine. There must be a law."

Transgender/trans
A person whose gender identity does not match with their gender assigned at birth. While this includes trans men and trans women, it can also include any and all nonbinary identities, though not everyone within these communities might choose to identify themselves as trans. Like the term *queer*, it is an adjective, and should not be used as a verb or a noun. A person can be transgender but is not "a transgender" or "transgendered."

"After working with trans youth for most of my time as a teacher, it wasn't until I was in my 30s that I realized I was likely transgender too."

Two-Spirit
A term that is closed to nonindigenous people (meaning that it cannot be used) that refers to a person who has both an internal masculine and feminine spirit. The identifying term was coined by American Indian and Alaska Native activists in 1990 to describe experiences that are centuries older and is used within many Indigenous communities today.

"Though two-spirit is a newer term, it is not a new concept, and the role, identity, and terminology is specific to Indigenous people in North America."

"Whoops, That's a Dog Whistle!"

A *dog whistle* is a word or phrase used by malicious and obstructive people to signal to other people of a similar mindset that they are on the same team. These are commonly code words that don't sound immediately alarming from the outside but have an insidious double meaning that often dehumanizes the intended target. In short, it's good to learn what these dog whistles are so we don't accidentally use them and so we can sort out quickly if we're talking to someone who isn't working in good faith.

While not all, many of the most pervasive anti-LGBT dog whistles are specific to trans individuals and experiences, as this is the group currently experiencing the most egregious bigotry nationwide.

- "Biological man/woman"
- "Natural-born man/woman"
- "Gender ideology"
- "Gender critical"
- "LGB rights"
- "Unwanted same sex attraction"

"Isn't 'queer' a slur?"

Nope.

Okay, fine, let's talk through it a bit more.

Though the word *queer* was used to describe someone who was weird, odd, or eccentric in the sixteenth century, right around the end of the 1800s, it became more frequently associated with homosexuality. It gained speed as a pejorative for another hundred years, but it was also used as a self-identifier for just as long. Our community started to work on concentrated efforts to reclaim *queer* for ourselves in the 1980s, as we're able to see clearly if we look back into the activist slogans, literature, and pop culture of the time.

Now if we look around from inside the LGBTQ+ community, the term is inescapable. Younger generations have become especially fond of it, and it is much harder to find someone who is offended by it than not. So why is that? Well, first, it's a super helpful umbrella term in a time where our acronym is getting unmanageably long. I have written a whole book about this topic and I'm still not quite sure where to stop when I'm typing it. Is it LGBT? LGBTQ+? LGBTQIA2SP+? Plus, it's pretty hard to pronounce. I much prefer "queer" to "Luhguhtuhbehquahplus."

There are, of course, quite a few people from within the LGBTQ+ community who don't want the term used to describe them, which is more than fair, but that doesn't mean it shouldn't be used at all, especially if someone is using it to describe their own life and identity. There are as many ways to be queer and to use queer language as there are queer people!

Notes from the Queer Teacher Survival Guide

On the Word "Queer"

"I don't like that word, I don't want to use it, and you can't use it for me."

That's totally fair! You are the only one who can decide what words are for you as an individual, but let's take just a moment for some transparent self-reflection and ask ourselves why this word specifically makes us uncomfortable:

Is it because *queer* is a term that has been historically used as a slur against us?

(Continued)

> If that's the case, I would argue that I can't think of a single identifying word in our community that hasn't been used as a slur. Many of us were born late enough that *queer* had vanished completely from bully vernacular, but we heard *lesbian*, *gay*, and *trans* with the same amount of venom. People who hold hate in their heart against us will always have a way of making the way a word is used FEEL like a slur no matter what it is. If we cross out all the words ever hurled at us, we won't have any left.
>
> Is it because we don't like that it's a term that feels "othering"?
>
> *Queer* is a word that has historically meant a separation, an oddness, a weird and slanted existence in margins, and it goes against seamless assimilation into a cisgender and heterosexual world. To put it bluntly, that's sort of the point. Frankly, the weirdos are your siblings too! We deserve love and belonging even when we don't try to erase ourselves into systems. Queer history means honoring the ancestors who were throwing bricks at Stonewall and marching against police dogs for us to have the right to take breath into our bodies now, and their "othering" was as central to their existence as it is for us today.
>
> Ultimately, you might have your own negative personal or historical association with it, so no worries at all if you still choose not to use it to describe yourself. No one can tell anyone else how to identify, but we also can't assert our personal feelings about identity onto anyone else. Queer is historically linked with us, with or without our permission.

Why Any of This Matters

PART I

CHAPTER ONE

A Brief and Recent History of the Author

Once a Teacher…

Before I knew anything else about myself, I knew I was a teacher.

When I give talks about my experience as an openly transgender educator, this is always how I start. A lot of teachers understand this feeling I think – of knowing practically out of the womb that there was something pulling them into the classroom. My knowing settled in my heart when I was right on the edge of leaving high school. As an incoming senior, I didn't have solid college plans yet, but I knew how I liked to spend my time. I was a reader and a storyteller, scribbling fiction in the margins of my SAT prep book and leaving homework uncompleted so I could demolish another YA paperback before bed. I didn't love school, but I did love English, and even though I was unreliable with assignments and exams, I was lucky to have a series of teachers who recognized and nurtured the fire I was carrying around with me.

But 12th grade was different. Where before I'd had teachers who saw me and made room for my differences, Mr. Willis[i] did not. He belittled my weird interpretations of classic poems, scolded me in front of my peers when I forgot my homework, and looked right through

---

[i] Name has been changed to a different person I don't like.

me when I raised my hand during class discussions. Suddenly, I didn't like English anymore. I stopped completing assignments that otherwise would have ignited me. I came into class late after lunch with bags of fast food. I stopped raising my hand.

One day, I realized that I was letting a single person ruin the only thing I loved, and that was when I started to really get how powerful a teacher could be.

A lot of teachers have a story about the "one teacher" who inspired them to get into the profession, who taught them just how influential and motivating the right adult presence can really be. I have that story too, but for slightly different reasons.

I got my shit together and got into college, studied hard, and worked as a writing tutor as I ran summer composition workshops. Once I got my credential, I was hired at the very first school to give me an interview. I came in early and left late every day for more than 10 years. I was convinced, top to bottom, that I would retire at 65 out of the same room I walked into at 21.

But that's not what happened.

What happened next is why I'm sitting here, writing this book, instead of unit mapping *Frankenstein* and scoring midterms.

More than a decade into my career and my very heterosexual marriage, I realized, quite out of nowhere, that I was probably trans.

Teachers do this a lot too – we forget to develop and explore our own identities, because we're always busy nurturing someone else's. There's no time for wondering who you are, what you like, and what you want, because it's a lot safer and easier to put a denim jacket on over a sundress and hold emotional space for teenagers. Yes, we self-abandon in the service of others, but also because it is exceptionally frightening to center and ask questions about ourselves.

I'm going to get through this next part quickly, because it still makes me very sad, and I'm making a concentrated effort not to spend too much time centering on trans pain in this book. There are a lot of books that do that – they make the whole of a trans person's story into a tragedy and turn a spotlight onto our misery. I understand why. Our pain is novel and interesting, and it is easier to empathize with someone when you can share a smidge of their suffering, but it also feels like we aren't worth listening to unless we're in pain. There are a lot of organizations who don't want me to speak on their panels or at their events unless I'm willing to relive that pain. I'm not interested in that.

So here we go.

In my time at my school after discovering that I was queer, quite a few things happened:

- I became the advisor for the queer student group on campus.
- I helped curate and develop a LGBTQ+ library in my classroom with children's books, books for parents, books with queer characters, fantasy books, science fiction books, books in four different languages, comic books, coloring books, and books about understanding queer history, identity, and culture.
- I started making videos about my gender transition and putting them on the Internet.

Someone who isn't a transgender teacher living and working in a conservative corner of the country might not understand that last one, but it's the part of this journey that I regret the least. I've never experienced extreme isolation like what I felt as the sole openly trans educator in my district of almost 50,000 students. I wanted to know who else was feeling what I was feeling. There were more of us than I thought.

As my audience grew, so did my precautions. I only filmed when I wasn't working. If I was ever in my classroom, there was nothing behind me that could identify my school. I didn't speak poorly of my community or my administrators or my students. In class, I kept talk about my own life to a minimum. I advocated for students, but my curriculum stayed in lock step with my colleagues. As a teachers' union representative, I knew how even a toe out of line could end a teacher's career if they were already a visible target.

It didn't matter.

Parents, but never of my own students, started bringing complaints to district higher-ups faster than I could respond to them. I shouldn't be on social media, they said. It was inappropriate for me to "share my pronouns" on the first day of school, they argued. The complaints were dismissed as quickly as they appeared, but it was only a matter of time for something to find footing.

Ultimately, it was the books that did it.

My classroom was one of the inaugural education spaces targeted by the first wave of twenty-first century "book banning." Someone from the community forwarded a list of titles in my library to a far-right entertainment news network. In the list of almost 300 books, they found two[ii] with material they opposed. So, one morning, I woke up to an article on the front page of one of the most visited websites in the conservative world that spelled out my deadname,[iii] where I worked, and allegations about my intentions with children that are too depraved and horrifying to repeat here.

In the months that followed, the harassment I faced at school ballooned to a level that became unsustainable. After a bomb threat, countless phone calls, three district email addresses flooded with hate, parent and community-organized protests and social media doxing, and one snail-mailed handwritten all-caps letter all the way from Kentucky, I was done.

I handed in my resignation two years after I came out as trans and left classroom teaching for good.

The Letters After Our Names

Books like this don't usually have detailed author biographies right out of the gate. In my time reading professional development literature, they're usually drafted by people with a series of very impressive letters after their name, but who these people actually are is a mystery outside

---

[ii] The books were *Juliet Takes a Breath* and *This Book Is Gay*.

[iii] If you missed the glossary, this refers to the name a trans person is given at birth that they no longer use. It is dangerous and unkind to share a trans person's deadname without their permission, as it opens them up to the potential for anti-trans harassment and violence.

of a short bullet-pointed list of where they earned the extra letters. That's not what's going to happen here. In this book, I'm going to spend a lot of time reiterating what we hear about marginalized experiences all the time: listen to the people who have lived them.

We can't argue that "representation is important" and then indulge in some weird "death of the author" when we're learning about these experiences for ourselves. That's bananas. What follows in these pages are ideas and advice that come from hard-won lived experience in the classroom and as a trans person navigating a startlingly unfriendly world, and there is no way to separate this knowledge and perspective from the person who survived it. There is no post-secondary program, no doctoral thesis, that will hand someone a more ironclad ethos here.

And transparently, we put a ton of stock into institutional knowledge, but those institutions work *really* hard to keep us out. I'm one of an estimated 7% of transgender people who have a degree higher than a bachelor's,[1] which is about half the national average. There is no data on the number of trans people with PhDs, but it's likely to be vanishingly small. Even if trans people were as equally represented among doctorate holders as they are in the general population, that would amount to less than 1% of the 2% of Americans who hold that distinction.

Even a number that high is unlikely, as trans people are much more likely to suffer the kinds of economic, emotional, and social distress that keep us far, far away from the kind of financial stability necessary to make it that far.

Really, for many of us, traditional markers of academic and professional success can suck an egg. We have, historically, been left out to dry by the same institutions that we are now expected to use to legitimize our voices. For example, in medicine and social work, up until 1973, the DSM[iv] classified homosexuality as a mental illness,[2] and it wasn't until

---

[iv] The *Diagnostic and Statistical Manual of Mental Disorders* published by the American Psychiatric Association. It is currently in its fifth edition and is the most common centralized diagnostic tool used by health professionals in the United States.

2013 that they reclassified us trans people away from what they long called "gender identity disorder."[3]

So yeah, we're good.

Who Is Worth Listening To

When I was in your position, reading a book like this to see if there was anything I could realistically use in my classroom, there was only one part of someone's biography that ever mattered to me: how long had they been in the classroom?

Because unless someone had really put in the hours, spending year after year attempting and failing and retrying and tweaking their own pedagogy, I wasn't interested. Too many authors, too many trainers, and too many administrators had spent a year or two with their toes dipped in and believed with their whole chest that they had something to offer to me.

Come back when you're so burned out and beaten down that you try to unlock your car with your classroom keys, please and thank you.

My trauma as a trans person may have made headlines and earned me a platform, but the entirety of my life made me a teacher and built the confidence and credibility I'm cashing in now.

I spent the entirety of my adult life giving everything to my school and my students. In this book, I will tell you everything I can about how to build an environment where students with identities like mine can survive and grow, but being trans is not the beginning and end of my own story. I wasn't just a "trans teacher."

Before that was the box built around me…

I coached our academic decathlon for 5 years and watched underestimated students take home trophies the school had never earned before.

I built an international curriculum for a film history class from scratch, during a pandemic, and piloted it from my living room.

I chaperoned every single school dance, holding cheap plastic breathalyzers up for hundreds of teenagers and swaying on the edge of the dance floor with a paper plate stacked high with Costco cookies.

I pretended that I had grading to do and stayed late with students whose parents forgot to pick them up at the end of the day.

I stood on the 50-yard line at football games with the other teachers (and left before the last kick to beat the traffic home).

I took buses of students to museums to hear about the Holocaust, to colleges to hear once-in-a lifetime speakers, to New York to see Broadway musicals. I collected permission slips and bus money. I drove a van full of hungry teenagers to a CVS in the middle of the night, hundreds of miles from home, and turned the windshield wipers on when one of them wouldn't climb down off the hood to go back to the hotel.

I had teacher friends. We played Dungeons and Dragons on the weekend and had a tradition after graduation every year where we wore matching paper crowns and ate with our hands at Medieval Times.

I wasn't just a teacher. I was a *teacher*.

I don't know if you will trust me, but I know I would trust me. I think that's enough.

Notes

1. Durso, Laura E., Rodrigo Heng-Lehtinen, Jody L. Herman and Sandy E. James. "Early Insights: A Report of the 2022 U.S. Transgender Survey." National Center for Transgender Equality, February 2024. https://transequality.org/sites/default/files/2024-02/2022%20USTS%20Early%20Insights%20Report_FINAL.pdf

2. Francine Russo, "Where Transgender Is No Longer a Diagnosis," Scientific American, February 20, 2024, https://www.scientificamerican.com/article/where-transgender-is-no-longer-a-diagnosis/

3. "Gender Dysphoria Diagnosis," A Guide for Working With Transgender and Gender Nonconforming Patients, American Psychiatric Association, 2024. https://www.psychiatry.org/psychiatrists/diversity/education/transgender-and-gender-nonconforming-patients/gender-dysphoria-diagnosis#:~:text=With%20the%20publication%20of%20DSM%E2%80%935%20in%202013%2C%20%E2%80%9Cgender,%2C%20medical%2C%20and%20surgical%20treatments

CHAPTER TWO

A Brief and Recent History of LGBTQ+ Issues in the Classroom

Finding the Beginning

Months after I had said goodbye to my last classroom full of students and left to start a new life miles away from the only school in which I had ever taught, my husband and I were invited to a very fancy lunch with a stylish couple. It was the sort of restaurant that served flower petals on top of microscopic salads, and I was picking at a suspicious bit of vegetation with a chilled fork when one of them used a brief silence to ask a question I'd gotten used to:

"So, where did this all start, do you think? The anti-gay stuff in schools, I mean?"

Where did "this all" start?

"This all" was hard to wrap my brain around, even now, even with the safety of distance and time between me and the scariest few years of my life.

When I started working on LGBTQ+ equity in public schools, I was barely 22, had zero idea that I was transgender, and was showing up to work every day in heels, chunky belts that squeezed my dangerously thin waist, and aggressively feminine dangly earrings. Like many people in my situation, I felt an invisible but undeniable tug into conversations about queer issues. I had strong opinions about marriage equality (still three or four years before Obergefell[i]) and jumped at the chance to attend our local LGBT Center's series on trans student rights. Even though we were still far behind in my district, early conversations about the changes we could be making for the benefit of queer students were relatively easy. Pushback was rare, parents and colleagues were casually curious and interested in ways they could help, and the general trajectory of LGBTQ+ acceptance seemed to be on the rise. After all, "Don't Ask, Don't Tell"[ii] had just been repealed, and Macklemore's "Same Love" was the song of the summer. I was scheduling productive meetings with the superintendent of our district and making real progress in the passing of inclusive, long-overdue school board policies. Progress seemed inevitable and unstoppable.

It wouldn't last.

Why Is It Always Kids?

Whenever there's a culture war brewing and dark clouds begin to gather, those who are looking for a good place to draw a starting line for moral panic will usually begin with inventing some looming (but always invisible) threat to children. Kids are the perfect tools for nefarious social purposes, because we have a deep-seated instinct to protect them, and we're willing to do whatever it takes to keep them safe from anything that might want to do them harm. "We must protect the children!" has been a rallying cry to mask ignorance and hate even before it was used to resist

---

[i] *Obergefell v. Hodges* is the 2015 Supreme Court decision that established the fundamental right to marry for same-sex couples in the United States by both the Due Process Clause and the Equal Protection Clause of the Fourteenth Amendment of the Constitution.

[ii] "Don't Ask, Don't Tell" (DADT) was an official United States policy that barred nonheterosexual people from serving openly in the military. Established by the Clinton administration in 1994, it was repealed in September 2011.

the desegregation of schools[1] throughout the 1950s and instigate an ocean of contrived fear during the "satanic panic"[iii] just a few decades later.

In fact, it's an argument that has been used with such frequency that it crossed over to the realm of parody, finding its way into the animated profit of cultural zeitgeist, *The Simpsons*, when the reverend's wife Helen Lovejoy finds her perfect maxim in the fight for a town-wide ban on the sale and consumption of alcohol: "Won't somebody please think of the children?"

Back in the real world, children are also the perfect distractions from more pressing and immediate national concerns; it's simply easier to win a manufactured emotional battle when you're losing a larger political war. Recently, when the State of Florida found itself on the business end of a teacher staff shortage,[2] Governor Ron DeSantis prioritized and passed HB 1557,[3] more widely known as the "Don't Say Gay" bill, to solve a problem that didn't exist: the exposure of school children in kindergarten through third grade to developmentally inappropriate materials on sexuality. The bill opened floodgates in Florida and across the country that resulted in an environment of shame and fear for educators and students, unquestionably energized anti-LGBTQ+ policy makers, and inspired expansions and additions all the way up through twelfth grade. During that same timeframe, no bills were proposed or passed to put a single new enthusiastic and qualified teacher in a single Florida classroom.

This tactic isn't strictly relegated to the world of education. The State of Texas found itself in the same position as Florida around the same time, but with its eyes trained in a different direction. While voters were

---

[iii]"Satanic Panic" is a phrase used to describe a period of time (primarily during the 1980s and early 1990s) where there was a spike in unsubstantiated claims of devil-worship, ritualistic abuse, and the moral corruption of children stemming from influences as diverse as the tabletop game Dungeons and Dragons to musicians such as Judas Priest and Marilyn Manson.

busy sounding the alarm around affirming care for transgender kids,[4] they were much less likely to focus on Texas' ranking as 45th in the country for access to healthcare,[5] with the highest uninsured rate in the country[6] and spiking shortages of doctors and nurses.[7] Invented problems are just much easier to solve.

The "big" issues, in education and beyond, take money and time, and there are much clearer measurable outcomes of success. Are test scores going up? Are class sizes going down? Are more students graduating? Are they pursuing degrees in higher education? Are we returning to pre-pandemic attendance levels? Do we have enough counselors to support the students who need them?

When the problems lawmakers and community advocates focus on are largely invented, rely on scare tactics around "protecting children," and tend to zero in primarily on how an environment "feels," the outrage shifts away from issues with large impact and tangible outcomes and instead settles on scapegoating communities who already exist in the margins.

Of course, schools have also been the eye of the storm because young people themselves are often the trailblazers of social change. Student-led protests and movements are born from both the internal adolescent struggle for autonomy and the historic lack of respect and power they hold within their world.

Way back in 1969, young people across the country won the right to free speech in public schools when *Tinker v. Des Moines* determined that students do not "shed their constitutional rights to freedom of speech or expression at the schoolhouse gate"[8] after 13-year-old Mary Beth Tinker and a handful of her peers wore black armbands to protest the Vietnam War. From staying seated during the Pledge of Allegiance to walking out during graduation addresses, students have been freely exercising this right for years, and it makes the people who would rather they exist only as silent imagined victims *exceptionally* nervous.

Here the Whole Time

The primary argument against finding room in school culture and curriculum for LGBTQ+ inclusion and representation has been that it is "developmentally inappropriate" for children to be engaged in conversations about sexuality and gender. But if you pull the Scooby Doo mask off the way we've been building and operating schools for hundreds of years, it becomes clear that the very scary Gender and Sexuality has been here the whole time, just dressed in more familiar clothes.

Classrooms from kindergarten through secondary place a heavy emphasis on gender and even heterosexuality right from the jump. From our very first encounter with school, we're taught to line up in boys' lines and girls' lines, and teachers address us collectively in a binary without thinking about why. Educators default to "Good morning, boys and girls," drawing a linguistic line right down the middle of us. We're learning how to relate to each other, how to make friends, and how to share, but all beside an overpowering narrative that is drawn for us: you are on one team, and half of your classmates are on the other.

Bathrooms, the setting for many fights about equity and access for transgender students, are entirely gender neutral when a child is at home. At school, bathrooms are now another setting where the teams are split, and those divisions become self-selected and continually reinforced as students develop. Teachers, faced with any classroom physical task (hoping to both lighten their own load and bump up the participation and autonomy of their students), seem to always ask: "Can I get a couple of big strong boys to help me with these desks?"

As students cross from the relative simplicity of elementary into the more treacherous social waters of middle and high school, expectations of gender remain. While many campuses are rightfully leaning away from strictly heterosexual and gender-typical expectations around social events such as homecoming and prom, it's still common to see students barred from attendance with same-sex dates,[9] as well as teens of all genders and sexualities kept away from celebrating with their peers when their outfits don't fit within anticipated gender norms.[10–12]

Though rarer (but not quite uncommon), campuses sometimes take their commitment to centering gender much more seriously. As of 2020, 18.8% of public schools still had uniform requirements, many of which require different norms for dress by gender.[13] There are public schools that, rather than offering the student body a singular option for graduation regalia, compel a segregated ceremony with separate color options by gender, with divorced seating to match.[14] In my own high school experience, which was (transparently) served partially in the district where I then spent the entirety of my career teaching, we hosted a traditional "spirit week" called "Battle of the Sexes." It went down about as maturely as you would expect with a slow devolution from cute pink and blue T-shirts and headbands to sexist chants and suggestively themed snacks that somehow snuck undetected past the school's activities director: free hot dogs one day for boys and donuts the next day for girls. I'm still not sure how that one happened.

And though much of the contemporary noise making surrounding classroom reading material focuses on attempted "indoctrination" from libraries and teachers who offer LGBTQ+ selections for students, there is never any acknowledgment that students almost exclusively encounter messaging that paints only one acceptable life path: a cisgender and heterosexual one. My own former school district offers 142 novel and play options for English language arts classrooms for ninth through twelfth grade.[15] Of those, from *Romeo and Juliet* to *A Tale of Two Cities* to *Siddhartha*, 132 feature at least one heterosexual marriage or romance. Only three titles, *A Separate Peace* (1959), *Billy Budd* (1924), and *The Picture of Dorian Gray* (1890), offer a whisper of homosexual (but never overt) subtext. In all three cases, the even lightly implied gay characters die by the final pages. The complete list features not a single sapphic[iv] romance or trans character.

[iv] "Sapphic" refers to relationships and/or romance between women, taken from the celebrated ancient Greek poet Sappho.

Teachers, arguably the most influential adults a young person will encounter outside of their immediate family system, also have a long and established history of modeling gender and sexuality norms, even overtly, within their classrooms. When I was catching the most heat in my community for introducing myself at the beginning of the year with my pronouns, a science teacher colleague of mine hosted a gender reveal for her unborn child in the central courtyard of our campus. Surrounded by hundreds of her students, she dropped a pumpkin from the top of a staircase that smashed to bits on the pavement below, revealing blue-tinted squash viscera. It's a boy.

From principals to paraeducators, public displays of gender and sexuality have always been not just tolerated but celebrated. Photos of families that have blossomed from heterosexual partnerships clutter teacher desks across the country, and students have been catching glimpses of wedding photo and family portrait desktop backgrounds for years, eyes fixed like hawks on the split second of intel they can gather between the minimizing of the PowerPoint screen and the shutting down of the overhead projector.

Elementary teachers announce engagements to enthusiastic fourth graders, pregnancies are celebrated and discussed casually as they develop throughout the school year, and adults in every corner of every campus in the country indulge daily in traditional aesthetic markers of gender identity that have zero tie to biological imperatives – painted nails, makeup, jewelry, heels, suits, ties, haircuts – with no concern that their choices have undue influence on the young people in their charge.

Queer people aren't pushing an agenda to insert gender and sexuality in schools – it's always been there. Feathers are ruffling not because these topics are suddenly appearing where before there was nothing, but because we are collectively desensitized when they don't challenge our existing paradigm. Essentially, "when you're accustomed to privilege, equality feels like oppression."[v]

---

[v] The origin of this phrase is unknown, but it's still true.

A Different Kind of Climate Change

When I first started "the work" more than 10 years ago, it seemed like progress was not only linear and steady but also inexorable. When I was introducing members of my staff to the reality of a queer and trans student presence on our campus, I was often their first introduction to the existence of LGBTQ+ experiences at all. If there were whispers of frustration or anger, they were silent to me. For the most part, their questions were logistical, not ideological.

The biggest pushback to new norms for trans students came from the foreign language department, who were perplexed only by the grammar. They were sure there was no gender-neutral pronoun in Spanish (there was, and is), and that was how a majority of those early conversations went for me: gently refocusing back to the individual well-being of students they knew and cared for.

I remember very clearly the first "high-profile" meeting I took with my principal in 2013, when I was barely 22. The first "out" trans student I'd ever had, a freshman, had come to me after a substitute teacher refused to use his name, instead opting for what was on the attendance sheet. The student tried to correct him, the class tried to correct him, and after three days with no change, he realized that taking it up to the principal was probably his last option, and he asked me to accompany him.

We were both nervous for the meeting; my principal was in the last year or two before his retirement, and he'd made his career in an especially conservative part of an already conservative county. As he was a career history teacher and championship football coach before becoming an admin, we had very few reasons to suspect he would be sympathetic. Something I've learned in years since then, however, is that people will always surprise you.

Not only was he supportive, but he was also pissed.

He had a young niece, he said, who spent three years insisting on a nickname that none of the rest of the family had ever heard before.

Instead of pushing back against it, they used it for her with zero questions or fuss. He didn't see why this should be any different. What does this guy care if his student wants to use a different name? It doesn't affect him. We do it all the time for the other kids. How were they ever supposed to practice being individuals if we shut them down all the time?

Before the hour was up, my principal had already marched down to that classroom and talked to the sub, who didn't call roll at all the next day. The original teacher returned, and life went on.

In the 10 years since, my principal retired, and two more have since cycled through his office. The trans freshman who was so scared to stand up for himself graduated both high school and college, and he's living a fully established adult life 400 miles away from the campus I expected would only continue to evolve.

But that's not what happened.

In fact, the aggressive national attitude shift we've seen in the last several years is the most intense backslide I've witnessed in LGBTQ+ advocacy over the course of my entire career. Now, it's very unlikely that real in-person experiences with real people are someone's introduction to the transgender community, and many opinions are firmly etched into stone before they're tested against reality.

The change rolled in like a fog: gentle and distant at first. Those of us on the front lines were too excited about our progress to slow down and notice the creeping signs that a backlash was coming. We learned that "visibility" was a first step, not an endgame, and it certainly wasn't going to keep us safe.

As the Water Begins to Warm

Though I was having a relatively "easy" time making changes and laying the foundation for a safe campus for LGBTQ+ students in my little pocket of public education in the 2010s, the country was already showing signs of unease that would ripple outward for years. And even with the sweeping positive progress in the way we treat queer Americans we've witnessed in our lifetime, there has never been a period of peace for us. In the 2022 US Trans Survey,[16] three quarters of the more than 92,000 transgender adult respondents admitted that they had an objectively bad time in school, experiencing routine mistreatment, harassment, bullying, and even physical attacks. We have always been denied the chance to dress the way we want, blocked from using school bathrooms and locker rooms, and demeaned and belittled by the adults who were supposed to be looking out for us.

And this isn't the first time in queer history where progress and regression have shared a spot on the timeline.

The passing of Title IX in 1972 in the United States, which assured that "no person in the United States shall, on the basis of sex, be excluded from participation in, be denied the benefits of, or be subjected to discrimination under any education program or activity receiving Federal financial assistance," debuted the same year as San Francisco's ban on anti-LGBT employment discrimination[17] and the very first Gay Pride in London.[18] That didn't stop the end of the decade from bringing us the Briggs Initiative: the very nearly successful ballot initiative that would have banned gay and lesbian teachers (and their supporters) from public classrooms. Temperatures and tolerance for LGBTQ+ issues are never a guarantee, and there are usually warning signs when positive change seems to come too quickly.

So, almost five years after I was pleasantly surprised by my principal, long after he retired and my first trans student had graduated and moved on, the pendulum began to swing.

The first alarms began to ring in North Carolina in 2016, just months before Donald Trump would win his bid for president. HB2, soon to be known as the infamous "bathroom bill," was the first successful policy of its kind, officially writing into North Carolina state law sweeping bans against municipal nondiscrimination policies, as well as forcing transgender students across the state to use restrooms and facilities in direct conflict with their lived identities.[19] With one stroke, thousands of young people were now thrown into immediate and unavoidable danger. Enforcing HB2 would require that public schools not only ignore, but directly violate, Title IX. Advocates and allies held their breath, watching and waiting.

Instead of fading, bills like HB2 only continued to grow. It wasn't until 2018, when Gavin Grimm, a high school student who had been denied access to the boys' restroom for his entire tenure at his Virginia public school, won his lawsuit in a US District court and was awarded $1.3 million in damages,[20] that LGBTQ+ advocates started breathing again.

Bills such as California's AB 1266 (the "School Success and Opportunity Act"), which "requires that pupils be permitted to participate in sex-segregated school programs, activities, and use facilities consistent with their gender identity, without respect to the gender listed in a pupil's records,"[21] were also being written and passed but not with nearly the same amount of attention and traction as their evil twins. Bathrooms were the battleground for several years, with the push and pull between groups of adults arguing at length regarding where teenagers were allowed to pee, reaching what felt like an endless fever pitch during the climax of every election cycle.

And this was the face of "the trans debate" in schools for years.

When schools shut down in March 2020, LGBTQ+ students were temporarily abandoned for other concerns, leaving the field empty for any new challenger who might want to seize the political opportunity when the conditions were just right again.

Enter DeSantis.

The Boiling Point

Despite the press's insistence to the contrary, I don't know a single educator who enjoyed teaching through the nationwide COVID-19 lockdown, especially if you were an advocate for LGBTQ+ students. While I certainly had a handful of high schoolers who seemed overjoyed by the extended time at home (I remember less than fondly a student joining our literature review Zoom from the chair of a ski lift), most queer students find an exceptional amount of reprieve and sanctuary at school. The return to the classroom should have been a triumph, for both us and them. The time at home meant a gap for queer and trans issues in the news, and we were all ready to start fresh.

We wouldn't have peace for long.

Florida's "Parental Rights in Education" bill, which would soon adopt the much more fitting title "Don't Say Gay," mandated that classroom lessons "by school personnel or third parties on sexual orientation or gender identity may not occur in kindergarten through Grade 3 or in a manner that is not age appropriate or developmentally appropriate for students in accordance with state standards."[22] Essentially, Governor DeSantis's mandate started by covering something that might seem obvious: restricting sexually explicit materials from kindergarten classrooms (K–3). The kicker, of course, was that no one was teaching sexually explicit materials to kindergarteners. The bill was a temperature test: would we tolerate it? The branding was key, as it was sold as an empowering tool for parents, who were feeling more disempowered than ever after more than a year of endless and often contradictory COVID-19 education guidelines. "Parental rights in education" has a much better flavor than "disempowered kids and educators in education."

But again, this bill was solving a problem that didn't exist. No one in the state of Florida was sexualizing 6-year-olds with their curriculum in public school classrooms. There was no evidence that children were being victimized. "Parental rights in education" was the beginning of a language shift that stuck around much longer than most of us anticipated. Suddenly, acknowledging queer family structures, reading LGBTQ+ children's books, and displaying LGBTQ+ rainbow flags were "grooming." This insidious turn of events began the newest campaign to open the definition of "explicit and inappropriate" to mean "us."

The language of the new law of the land was vague and seemed challenging to enforce. What counts as "developmentally appropriate"? Who would determine if the policy had been violated? Did acknowledging trans students or staff, or displaying a family photo, constitute "teaching" about gender identity and sexual orientation? It was just nebulous enough, and the consequences were just severe enough (educators faced suspension and even a full revocation of their teaching licenses) to scare many teachers out of trying at all.

Proponents of the changes were quick to argue that we were overreacting and the bill wasn't telling us not to "say gay"; it was just keeping predators from taking advantage of the small and moldable minds of our most vulnerable and young students. Middle school and high school were still fair game. Nothing that escalated that narrative would progress from here.

Less than a year later, "Don't Say Gay" expanded up through twelfth grade.[23]

And the temperature rises.

Similarly empowered by the educational wild west that was the COVID-19 pandemic, the conservative action group Moms for Liberty found their footing first with mask mandates before they turned their eyes on books.

"Talking about sex, reading about sex – basically anything related to sex – is not needed in the lives of children." The words of Loretta Lowe, a parent in Chattanooga, Tennessee, who was readily buying what Moms for Liberty was selling. "I'm confident that the new policies will remove the grooming from the schools."[24]

And she wasn't alone.

This was where my intersection with the trajectory of anti-LGBTQ classroom sentiment became more of a high-speed head-on collision. My queer library, lovingly curated and grown by the students of our campus's Queer Student Alliance, found its way into the crosshairs of the culture war. Soon my own school board looked just like the rest of them. Holding me up as an example of deviance and delusion, parents looked me and my decades-long career in the face and said things like:

"When Flint chose it upon [himself] to place books containing graphic and sexual content in the classroom, [he] opened the door to pseudo-pornography. The information contained in these books is going to cause an increase in sexual activity, higher rates of STDs, pregnancy, and students putting themselves in harmful situations."[25]

I was, and still am, absolutely devastated.

If anything within the umbrella of LGBTQ+ now falls into the bucket of "inappropriate" and "sexually explicit" and being openly queer makes you a "groomer," language and identity begin to unravel. We have been living as the frog in a slowly boiling pot of water. It's only when it's too late to jump out that we realize what's been happening the whole time. Now that we are more collectively open to laws and attitudes that push us back into the margins, our identities and our lives are unfit for public consumption.

Thanks primarily to the efforts of Moms for Liberty, "Book banning in the United States (2021–present)" now has its own Wikipedia page.[26]

The Bright Side

Remember, we made a pledge not to lay too long on the hot pavement and of despair. Our story doesn't end here.

When children are kept from queer stories and queer people, from healthcare and sports and bathrooms and curriculum, all they really learn is shame, and the educational landscape is not barren of professionals who know that.

Whenever I need a pick-me-up, I remember that for every new anti-LGBTQ law or bill or insecure, attention-starved politician who springs from the ground, there are just as many (if not more) good and compassionate people working proactively to protect us.

As of 2024, close to half of the LGBTQ population lives in a state with laws prohibiting bullying on the basis of sexual orientation and gender identity, and more than half of us live in states with laws prohibiting discrimination in schools under the same circumstances.[27] States such as New Jersey, Illinois, Colorado, California, Nevada, Oregon, and Washington explicitly require LGBTQ inclusion in state curricular standards, and it's still a minority of states that are buying all the way into anti-LGBTQ school curriculum censorship.[28]

There's a lot of work to be done, but this isn't an impossible mountain. There are options aside from climbing into the shower fully clothed and listening to Alanis Morisette.

We can't give up. Not yet. There are still kids who need us.

Notes from the Queer Teacher Survival Guide

Keep an Eye on Your Blood Pressure

Reading about and experiencing how we're viewed and treated by our local, national, and global community is not just stressful, it's traumatic. We are traumatized actively when we open our newsfeeds and flinch at every headline that highlights the continued attack on our community. It's not natural to be so routinely confronted by psychological pain on such a tremendous scale. Where do you feel it in your body? Step away if you need to. Take a break. Remember that how we are used, hurt, and ignored is not who we are. We have community; we have support; we are recipients of love. When we show up for kids and live in our authenticity, we are not harming anyone. Hold compassion for yourself at every opportunity.

Notes

1. Egerton, John. "Walking into History: The Beginning of School Desegregation in Nashville." Southern Spaces, May 4, 2009, https://southernspaces.org/2009/walking-history-beginning-school-desegregation-nashville/

2. "Teacher and Staff Shortage." Florida Education Association, last updated September 2022, https://feaweb.org/issues-action/teacher-and-staff-shortage/

3. "What You Need to Know about Florida's 'Don't Say Gay' and 'Don't Say They' Laws, Book Bans, and Other Curricula Restrictions." National Education Association, 2022, https://www.nea.org/sites/default/files/2023-06/30424-know-your-rights_web_v4.pdf

4. Spoto, Maia. "Here's what to know about transition-related health care, which Texas has banned for children." The Texas Tribune, Updated December 3, 2024, https://www.texastribune.org/2023/03/24/texas-transgender-kids-transition-related-health-care/

5. "Health Care," Best States Rankings, U.S. News and World Report, accessed June 3, 2024, at https://www.usnews.com/news/best-states/rankings/health-care

6. Novack, Sophie. "American Health Care is Broken, Especially in Texas. What can we do about it?" Texas Observer, September 10, 2019, https://www.texasobserver.org/american-health-care-is-broken-especially-in-texas-what-can-we-do-about-it/

7. Petrie, Bonnie. "Texas Primary Care Doctor Shortage Spikes During the Pandemic; Rural Texans Hit Hardest." Texas Public Radio, November 17, 2021, https://www.tpr.org/public-health/2021-11-17/texas-primary

8. "*Tinker v. Des Moines* - Landmark Supreme Court Ruling on Behalf of Student Expression," ACLU, February 22, 2019, https://www.aclu.org/documents/tinker-v-des-moines-landmark-supreme-court-ruling-behalf-student-expression#:~:text=February%2022%2C%202019-,Tinker%20v.,protest%20the%20war%20in%20Vietnam

9. Nardino, Meredith, "Prom Discrimination: Student Stories from All 50 States." Do Something, April 26, 2019, https://dosomething.org/article/prom-discrimination-stories

10. Diaz, Jaclyn, "A Nashville Senior was Banned from Prom for a Suit, so a Local Business Stepped In." NPR, April 25, 2023, https://www.npr.org/2023/04/25/1171695996/nashville-senior-banned-from-prom-suit-dress

11. Yurcaba, Jo, "Florida Teen Says she was Denied Entry to Prom for Wearing a Suit." NBC News, May 15, 2024, https://www.nbcnews.com/nbc-out/out-news/florida-teen-says-was-denied-entry-prom-wearing-suit-rcna152440

12. Power, Shannon, "Transgender Teen Denied Entry to Prom for Wearing Dress." Newsweek, April 10, 2024, https://www.newsweek.com/transgender-teen-prom-dress-alabama-lgbtq-1888839

13. "School Uniforms," Fast Facts, National Center for Education Statistics, Retrieved July 1, 2024 from https://nces.ed.gov/fastfacts/display.asp?id=50

14. Phillips, Jessi, "Do Gendered Graduation Gowns Alienate Trans and Nonbinary Students?" Michigan Public Radio Network, December 21, 2023, https://www.wmuk.org/wmuk-news/2023-12-21/do-gendered-graduation-gowns-alienate-trans-and-nonbinary-students

15. "CUSD HIGH School Board Approved Curriculum and Literature." Capistrano Unified School District, Last Updated August 2018, https://www.capousd.org/documents/District/Our-District/Cultural-Proficiency/Classroom-Curriculum/2306216908665050370.pdf

16. Durso, Heng-Lehtinen, Herman and James, "Trans Survey."

17. "The 1970s," Timeline, SF Gay History, Retrieved July 1, 2024 from https://www.sfgayhistory.com/timeline/the-1970s/

18. Murphy, Gillian, "The Gay Liberation Front." The London School of Economics and Political Science, April 25, 2023, https://blogs.lse.ac.uk/lsehistory/2023/04/25/the-gay-liberation-front/

19. Miller, Hayley, "Five Things to Know About North Carolina's Newest, Radical Anti-LGBT Law." The Human Rights Campaign, March 24, 2016, https://web.archive.org/web/20160514065936/http://www.hrc.org/blog/five-things-to-know-about-north-carolinas-newest-radical-anti-lgbt-law

20. "Gloucester County School Board to Pay $1.3 Million to Resolve Gavin Grimm's Case," Press Releases, ACLU, August 26, 2021, https://www.aclu.org/press-releases/gloucester-county-school-board-pay-13-million-resolve-gavin-grimms-case

21. "Protections for LGBTQ+ Students: AB 1955." California Department of Education, Last Updated on July 15, 2024, https://www.cde.ca.gov/ci/pl/ab-1955-sum-of-prov.asp

22. O'Connor, Lydia, "Gov. Ron DeSantis Signs Florida's 'Don't Say Gay' Bill Into Law." Huffpost, March 28, 2022, https://www.huffpost.com/entry/ron-desantis-signs-dont-say-gay-bill-florida_n_6227adfbe4b004a43c10cb11

23. Contorno, Steve, "Florida Bans Teaching of Gender Identity and Sexual Orientation Through 12th Grade." CNN, April 19, 2023, https://www.cnn.com/2023/04/19/politics/florida-bans-teaching-gender-identity-sexual-orientation/index.html

24. Jedeed, Laura, "Moms for Liberty Has Created Nightmares for Schools Across the Country." The New Republic, May 31, 2022, https://newrepublic.com/article/166373/moms-liberty-schools-nightmare-midterms

25. Breaux, Collin, "Capo Unified Community Discusses Anti-LGBTQ Bigotry, Sexually Explicit Books Following San Juan Hills Bomb Threat." Picket Fence Media, December 16, 2022, https://www.picketfencemedia.com/capo-unified-community-discusses-anti-lgbtq-bigotry-sexually-explicit-books-following-san-juan-hills-bomb/article_60a40ec3-69a2-5b28-bb13-d14f0d66f226.html

26. "Book banning in the United States (2021–present)." Wikipedia, last modified December 26, 2024, https://en.wikipedia.org/wiki/Book_banning_in_the_United_States_(2021%E2%80%93present).

27. "Safe Schools Laws," Equality Maps, Movement Advancement Project, last modified July 12, 2024, https://www.lgbtmap.org/equality-maps/safe_school_laws

28. "LGBTQ Curricular Laws," Equality Maps, Movement Advancement Project, last modified January 4, 2024, https://www.lgbtmap.org/equality-maps/curricular_laws

CHAPTER THREE

A Brief and Not-So-Recent History of LGBTQ+ Teaching

Life in a Fishbowl

Teaching has always been a uniquely public profession in a way that's hard to understand unless you've found yourself on the business end of the consequences. Every educator has had a moment of uncomfortable pondering in the checkout line as we weigh the pros and cons of attempting to buy a six pack of hard ciders less than a mile from our campus.

Unless employed by a private school that compels its staff to sign a personal "morality clause," there are no laws or policies that keep us from living completely within the bounds of reasonable adult free will, but there are few of us who do. This is because we see ourselves (as does the public) as living our life in a kind of fishbowl, even when we're well past the last bell and miles from the inside of our classrooms. There are few jobs that require someone to think about how they're perceived when they aren't on the clock, especially in the same way that teachers do. This is because we think of teachers as moral guardians – shepherds who are expected to model what it means to live a representative life for the benefit of our students. Because we spend time in front of children, the expectation is that we live as if they are always watching and that we consider what each of their families might think of our choices for ourselves.

This, of course, is bonkers.

The only other career that comes close to operating within the same full-time moral monitoring would be a member of the clergy, and at least they have only one religion to consider at a time.

In my early teaching program, all the fresh-off-the-lot baby teachers were given the same advice: live carefully. Keep your social media private, don't let anyone catch you with a red Solo cup in your hand, think twice about the bikini you're wearing in that group photo, and never (ever) have loud opinions, especially political ones.

And it's not as if that advice came from nowhere. Plenty of teachers have found themselves in hot water for seemingly innocuous reasons with districts who have weak unions and strict personnel policies. Many of those districts don't pair the standards they set for teachers with equal expectations for students and families, who are much more protected under local and national free speech laws than educators. Research tells us that one in five teachers have been subject to online bullying or harassment at the hands of a student or parent.[1] The party line here for administrators and teacher trainers has been that if teachers are careful about what they make available to the children in their charge, they should be safe. There should be no reason for concern if an educator just lives right, and lives privately.

But I vividly remember the experience of a colleague only a year into my first position. She was a model teacher with a Pinterest-style meticulously labeled room. She sported shoulder-length blonde hair, a wardrobe made almost exclusively of denim jackets and modest white dresses, and a completely locked-down personal life. There wasn't a single thing transpiring in her life that made its way into classroom discussion, and she was proud of her ability to hold strict social boundaries with her ninth and tenth grade students. Even her desktop background was a highly saturated stock image of a Tahitian beach, ensuring that anyone savvy enough to catch a glance of it learned exactly nothing about what she did with her time after 3 p.m.

It didn't matter.

She made the mistake of eating dinner in a town almost 15 miles from our campus, and one of her students spotted her. That student snapped a photo, uploaded it to Snapchat while she was waiting to be seated with her family, and it was on every single phone screen in her classroom the next morning, with the same caption highlighted in the center:

"Ms. L seen dining with mystery guy??"

The mystery guy was, of course, not a mystery to anyone whose business it was to know; he was her husband. It was ridiculous, it was silly, and it was nothing. That didn't mean it wasn't the center of whispered discussion for days. It also brought up a question that stayed with me long after the rumors dissolved into the ocean of the school year:

"If she isn't safe, what the hell is going to happen to me?"

In the Beginning

Administrators and families seeing teachers (and school staff as a whole) as role models is not a bad standard. In fact, it's a natural one. This is always how we've learned, since well before we built classrooms and filled them with students. Children watch their parents, and every other adult in their lives, as they construct for themselves what they want their own adult reality to look like.

It's worth wondering why "role model" means to us that an adult a child interacts with at school has to take measures to hide parts of their day-to-day life before and after the bell. It's likely that other adults, such as the child's parents and extended family, do not.

Why does "role model" not immediately mean "modeling healthy boundaries with work" or "how to work through challenging emotions under pressure," instead of "lives the way individual members of the community believe a morally upstanding citizen ought to live?"

For that answer, we have to pull the camera back just a bit.

For a long time, education in the United States looked a bit different than it does today and doesn't quite fit the picture of the romanticized, traditional, one-room schoolhouse we've built up in our collective consciousness.

Throughout the 1600s and 1700s, when the states were still loosely organized and mostly under British control, those worthy of schooling were divided very much along lines of class, race, and gender. There were no public schools. If a child received an education at all, it was because the community constructed a school, usually funded by the church, and staffed it on their own. Wealthier Americans sent their children to well-funded boarding schools or set them up with in-home tutoring. Teachers were almost exclusively men, and children in rural areas or else born into poverty were losing the race before it even started.[23]

It wasn't until the 1800s, a few decades after the Founding Fathers argued that a successful union was possible only through a universally educated public, that public schools started to look possible. After some familiar arguments about rising taxes and bootstraps, "common schools" started popping up across the country. In addition to teaching the "three Rs" (that is, Reading, Writing, and Arithmetic), proponents of common schools won debates by highlighting the chance the public would now have to influence the "moral education" of our nation's youth. Instead of investing money in jails and courts to handle the fallout from high rates of poverty and crime, public schools could swoop in and educate children to become upstanding citizens.

Horace Mann, the architect and original advocate of public education in the United States, argued in 1840 that it was the duty of those overseeing education to "see that no teacher crosses its threshold, who is not clothed, from the crown of his head to the sole of his foot, in garments of virtue."[4]

And it's for this, the moral education of American children, is when we see the torch passed from men to women, who were argued by educational reformers as the natural choice for teaching the young people of the United States how to live good and productive lives, as well as all those very critical Rs.

Women's inherent lady-ness was cited and elevated as their primary qualifier. Girls are predestined to take on roles as caretakers at home, so why not also in the new public schools that were sweeping the nation?

Like a lot of current stereotyping, commonly held beliefs about the inherent "nurturing and moral character" of young women might sound like a compliment, but it's not. Western notions of a woman's place as the pure and chaste center of her household, as opposed to the strong and competent (though less ethically balanced) position of men, has always been rooted in misogyny. Though they would be excellent spiritual guides, it was argued, they would almost certainly have an impossible time managing unruly classrooms or setting boundaries with boys. Of course, it wasn't true. Anyone who has ever had a truly dedicated teacher of any gender knows that the bathroom they use before class has little to do with the quality of the lesson they deliver after.

But what was the more practical and material reason to employ women in such high numbers?

In the words of the Littleton School Committee of Massachusetts in 1849:

> "God seems to have made woman peculiarly suited to guide and develop the infant mind, and it seems...very poor policy to pay a man 20 or 22 dollars a month, for teaching children the ABCs, when a female could do the work more successfully at one third of the price."

So yes, they did pay them less. A lot less. Women who were hired to lead classes for the new common schools earned a third of the salary offered to men across the country. With limited employment options and the rare chance to further their own education, girls as young as 15 started taking on students, establishing classrooms, and setting the expectation that teaching is a "women's profession" to such a degree that we still haven't quite shaken it.

This is also when the fishbowl starts to form.

With schools becoming more common and accessible, towns large enough for a church also had a school, with at least one woman following close behind. And with women positioned as the virtuous authority of these schools, there were a host of rules imposed on their conduct. Some of those included tidbits such as these[5]:

- After 10 hours in school, teachers may spend their remaining time reading the Bible or other good books.
- Teachers who marry or engage in unseemly conduct will be dismissed.
- Teachers must be home between the hours of 8 p.m. and 6 a.m. unless attending a school function.
- Teachers may not travel beyond the city limits unless they have permission of the chairmen of the board.
- Teachers may not smoke, dye their hair, or dress in bright colors.
- Teachers may not ride in a carriage or automobile with any man unless he is their father or brother.
- Teachers must wear at least two petticoats, and dresses must not be any shorter than 2 inches above the ankles

There is no historical record of the position regarding jeans on Fridays.

And the Accusations Roll In

Okay, but what does this have to do with queer teachers?

We're getting there, but remember, homosexuality has been criminalized in the United States for most of its (white and European) history.

The moment the first Puritans touched buckled shoe to beach, they wrote laws imposing the death penalty on any of their neighbors who might be looking at each other just a little too long.[6] It wasn't until 2003, the same year that gave us *Finding Nemo* and the third *Lord of the Rings* movie, that the Supreme Court overturned the last of the laws in the United States that made "homosexual acts" a jailable offense.[7]

This didn't mean gay teachers just sprung out of the ground in 2004. We've always been here, and you can see us peeking out through history, though not always for cheerful reasons.

Take Lillian Hellman's 1934 play *The Children's Hour*. Though the play is fiction, it was based on a real 1810 account of two Scottish teachers accused by one of their students of having a lesbian affair. In the play, as in real life, the women have their lives and reputations ruined by the suggestion that they might love each other. Ninety-year-old spoilers ahead, but one of them doesn't make it to the curtain drop alive.

Again, the accounts in the play are made up, but the sentiment and circumstances were real. The stakes have always been astronomically high for teachers who have found their love and identity in direct odds with the prevailing cultural expectations of sexuality and gender, and rise in visibility has not, and does not, guarantee anyone the safety, dignity, and respect they deserve.

This became clear in the early red dawn of the 1950s, only a few short years after the end of the second World War. Afraid that communism and her twin sister atheism would worm their way into good clean American schools, federal officials started making some swift changes to public education in a way that would bruise us for much longer and deeper than the creeping threat of Soviet supremacy.

The weirder versions of this came with reforms like the addition of "under God" to the Pledge of Allegiance,[8] presidential physical fitness tests,[9] and the comeback of homework,[10] which had fallen out of fashion during the Great Depression. More nefarious was the rise of the House Un-American Activities Committee (HUAC), tasked with finding and rooting out the communist spies living silently and watchfully among the law-abiding citizens of the United States. This task included the "scrubbing" of American social and civic life, meaning that a series of laws and statutes were implemented nationwide limiting "vagrancy, sodomy, extramarital sex and loitering," making it easy for the police to target and arrest queer people living visible lives.[11]

This new moral panic came alongside a "Lavender Scare," where gay and lesbian government employees were hunted down and expelled from their jobs under the excuse that their "deviant" behavior made them more susceptible to blackmail at the hands of our nation's enemies.

Teachers, visible and vulnerable in their fishbowl, weren't exempt from this treatment either.

Though a purge of queer teachers began to unfold across the country, none was quite as vicious as the Johns Committee investigations in Florida from 1957 to 1963, where educators were interrogated, were fired, and often had their licenses revoked while being threatened with jail time and without due process, stemming from accusations often leveled against them by their own students. During that period, in one state alone, more than 100 teachers and professors lost their jobs.[12]

American kangaroo courts spent decades intimidating and eradicating LGBTQ+ influences from public life, using the threat of communism as grounds for ruining thousands of lives and reputations without any evidence that they were causing harm.

If the story ended there, if queer people let state-sponsored harassment and domestic terror keep us from living and loving as our full and complete selves, this would be a super-duper depressing book.

But I promise it's not.

> "Tomorrow is a funny word... We would have had to invent a new language, as children do, without words like tomorrow."
> —The Children's Hour

The Pie Heard 'Round the World

One Friday in Iowa in 1977, former beauty pageant winner and Florida Citrus Commission brand ambassador Anita Bryant was giving a press conference that was unceremoniously interrupted by a banana cream pie.

The pie was a response to Bryant's public campaign to defame and remove LGBTQ people from places of "public influence," both in Florida and across the United States. In the late 1970s, Florida was one of the few states that had passed an ordinance prohibiting discrimination in employment and housing, and that burned Anita Bryant's biscuit to such a degree that she became the face of the "Save Our Children" campaign to overturn it. During her time crossing the country speaking about her crusade, she made charming arguments such as "what these people really want, hidden behind obscure legal phrases, is the legal right to propose to our children that theirs is an acceptable alternate way of life"[13] and "the recruitment of our children is absolutely necessary for the survival and growth of homosexuality…for since homosexuals cannot reproduce, they must recruit, must freshen their ranks."[14] Because her campaign hinged on the "protection" of children, gay and lesbian teachers were often in her crosshairs.

But by this time, queer activism wasn't hidden or demure. Our community took up the fight for public opinion, boycotting Florida citrus and speaking against the rhetoric that was trying to push them back into the closet. Gay bars stopped serving screwdrivers and started mixing "Anita Bryants," swapping the OJ typically paired with vodka with apple juice. And one beautiful October day in Des Moines, gay activist Tom Higgins interrupted Bryant's press conference, one where she had been laying out her plans for her own "gay conversion" camp, by delivering a smuggled banana pie square in the face of a woman who was using all of the money, power, and influence to wipe him and his community out of the public consciousness.

"At least it was a fruit pie," Bryant said moments before she broke into prayer and tears.[15]

Though her fight for a repeal passed, it was reinstated later in the late 1990s. Bryant, however, was dropped from her ambassador role with Florida oranges, her marriage dissolved, she was roasted on late-night television by Johnny Carson until no venues would host her, she filed for bankruptcy, and has faded into obscurity back from whence she came. In 2021, her granddaughter came out as gay.[16]

So often we remember the villains but not the heroes. Tom Higgins, pie-tosser-in-chief, is often credited as the one who coined the phrase "gay pride" in his work as an activist in Minnesota. He and his friend Bruce Brockway, who had also attended the pieing, founded the Positively Gay Cuban Refugee Task Force, and with their community-sponsored gay refugees looking to resettle in the United States. He, like so many of our LGBTQ+ siblings, passed as a casualty of the AIDS epidemic in 1994.[17]

My Name Is Harvey Milk, and I'm Here to Recruit You

In 1978, only a year after the pie, and at the same time as the debut of the Cabbage Patch doll and *Grease*, a senator 3,000 miles from Bryant's campaign in Florida was attempting to craft a similar win for his political career in California.

John Briggs, a senator representing a part of California I lived in for most of my adult life, proposed Prop 6, more commonly known as the Briggs Initiative, aiming to ban gay and lesbian teachers, along with their allies, from California classrooms. Throughout his efforts, he made public statements arguing that homosexuality was a more damaging public menace than communism because it spread "like a cancer," and he claimed that there was a large and secret population of gay teachers working to victimize children.[18] The ballot measure highlighted the primary concern as "public homosexual activity or conduct," which he defined as "the advocating, soliciting, imposing, encouraging, or promoting of private or public homosexual activity directed at, or likely to come to the attention of schoolchildren and/or other employees."[19] Essentially, his argument was in line with Bryant's: children were in danger of being influenced and preyed upon by queer teachers, and they needed to be rooted out and expelled from classrooms as soon as possible.

The proposition sent ripples of fear across the state. Initial polling saw it passing with a similar margin to Bryant's initiative in Florida, with a vast majority of Californians in support of the gay purge.

Activists mobilized, speaking wherever they could about the dangers and realities of what Briggs was selling. And in June, recently elected San Francisco city supervisor (and the first openly gay man to hold elected office in California) Harvey Milk led the charge to turn the tide. In one of his most famous speeches, Milk, who began with "My name is Harvey Milk, and I'm here to recruit you," poking direct fun at the absurd claims of Briggs and Bryant, called for the support of President Jimmy Carter as he picked apart the claims of the people who were openly calling every queer person in the country degenerates and child predators.

"About six months ago," Milk said to the crowd that gathered around him on the steps of San Francisco's City Hall, "Anita Bryant in her speaking to God said that the drought in California was because of the gay people. On November 9, the day after I got elected, it started to rain."[20]

President Carter issued a statement against Prop 6, along with former President Gerald Ford and former California Governor Ronald Reagan. In November, three weeks before Harvey Milk was assassinated in San Francisco City Hall, the Briggs Initiative was defeated by California voters 58.4–41.6%.[21]

Queer Teachers Today

We live in a different world now, even if the parallels to the past are hard to stomach.

In 2005, the ACLU filed a claim on behalf of Diane Schroer, a retired US Army Colonel who applied, and was then rejected, from a role at Library of Congress' Congressional Research Service after they learned that she was transgender.[22] The case brought into question the scope of the Civil Rights Act of 1964, also known as Title VII, which bans employment discrimination in the United States on the basis of sex. Though the Library tried to argue that sex was "purely chromosomal," the court returned that "Title VII is violated when an employer discriminates against any employee, transsexual[i] or not, because he or she has failed to act or appear sufficiently masculine or feminine enough for an employer," explaining also that it's "well-established that, as a legal concept, 'sex' as used in Title VII refers to much more than which chromosomes a person has."[23]

In 2012, the Transgender Law Center argued a similar case for transgender veteran and former police detective Mia Macy, who was removed from consideration for a position with the federal Bureau of Alcohol, Tobacco, Firearms, and Explosives when the organization discovered that she was midway through a gender transition. The Macy decision added to Schroer's by involving the Equal Employment Opportunity Commission (EEOC), the federal agency responsible for interpreting and enforcing all US laws prohibiting employment discrimination. The EEOC ruled in Macy's favor, meaning that transgender and gender nonconforming people across the country have their protection in their corner should they ever need it.

In June 2020, the Supreme Court upheld that decision federally,[24] but it's always possible for them to reverse their decision, as they did for federal abortion protections in 2022.[25] If that were to become the case, there

---

[i] Some people use this term as a self-identifier today, but most of us do not. It's a good rule to not use it to describe anyone unless they have expressly asked for it.

are still 16 US states and 2 US territories as of 2024 that do not have explicit employment protections in the case of sexuality and gender identity.[26]

Nationally, protected or not, queer teachers are feeling the heat.

Deep in Florida's "Don't Say Gay" country, a teacher shortage is only being worsened by educators who would rather flee than face the uncertainty of their professional futures.[27] Others are being fired for reading books featuring queer characters.[28] Many more are avoiding the profession entirely, unsure of where to go from here.

This contemporary reality, when paired with the distant queer history that preceded it, is why queer educator voices are so important, and why books like these should be written by those of us who have spent our lives and careers in the arena, fighting not only for our students but for ourselves. We rely on our allies to carry the torch when we can't and keep it burning when the weight becomes unbearable, but we should always have the chance to speak for ourselves when we can. Because historically, powerful, ignorant, and malicious forces will do whatever they can to keep us silent.

Notes from the Queer Teacher Survival Guide

On Visibility

We talk so much about how good visibility is for our students that we often don't step back and ask how good visibility is for us. The truth is, no one is owed any part of you that you don't want to share, and not a single person is entitled to the full picture of your truth. You are who you are with or without it. You aren't "hiding" or "lying" if you choose to keep the personal details of your life away from the prying eyes of administration, your colleagues, or your students, in the same way that a student has no obligation to share those details with

(Continued)

you. We know that LGBTQ+ students are positively impacted when their identities are reflected by the adults they interact with at school, but that doesn't always make it safe or wise to "come out" in our place of work. Here are some pros and cons to "self-disclosure" that you might consider before you make this decision for yourself:

- **Pros:**
  - Deepens established trust and connections between you and the LGBTQ+ students on your campus
  - Represents a reality many queer kids don't see enough: that queer adults can safely and successfully make it to adulthood
  - Allows non-LGBTQ+ students to see that we are just as trustworthy, competent, and diverse as the cisgender and heterosexual adults in their lives
- **Cons:**
  - Opens you to threats against your personal safety, especially if you live in a state or region without employment protections
  - Sometimes results in harassment from students, families, and community members

No matter what you choose to disclose, remember that any pushback you experience is not the result of your moral character or a reflection of the energy and love that you bring to your job. You are part of a long history of educators who may have to fight to be seen, but you're not in that fight alone.

Notes

1. Marsh, Sarah, "Should Schools Do More to Protect Teachers from Cyberbulling?" The Guardian, May 21, 2014, https://www.theguardian.com/teacher-network/teacher-blog/2014/may/21/schools-protect-teachers-cyberbullying-online-abuse
2. Kober, Nancy and Diane Stark Rentner, "History and Evolution of Public Education in the US." Center on Education Policy, 2020, https://files.eric.ed.gov/fulltext/ED606970.pdf

3. "Historical Timeline of Public Education in the US," Reports, Race Forward, last modified in 2023, https://www.raceforward.org/reports/education/historical-timeline-public-education-us

4. "Teaching Timeline," Only A Teacher, PBS, accessed April 31, 2024, https://www.pbs.org/onlyateacher/timeline.html

5. Strauss, Valerie, "Rules for Teachers in 1872: No Marriage for Women or Barber Shops for Men." The Washington Post, June 2, 2011, https://www.washingtonpost.com/blogs/answer-sheet/post/rules-for-teachers-in-1872-no-marriage-for-women-or-barber-shops-for-men/2011/06/01/AGTSSpGH_blog.html

6. "Criminalization of Homosexuality in American History," LGBTQ+ People, Death Penalty Information Center, accessed May 3, 2024, https://deathpenaltyinfo.org/policy-issues/lgbtq-people/criminalization-of-homosexuality-in-american-history

7. Weinmeyer, Richard, "The Decriminalization of Sodomy in the United States," AMA Journal of Ethics, Virtual Mentor. 2014;16 (11):916–922, https://journalofethics.ama-assn.org/article/decriminalization-sodomy-united-states/2014-11

8. Little, Becky, "Why Eisenhower Added 'Under God' to the Pledge of Allegiance During the Cold War." History, June 22, 2022, https://www.history.com/news/pledge-allegiance-under-god-schools

9. Grieve, Victoria, "The Cold War in the Schools: Educating a Generation for World Understanding," Little Cold Warriors: American Childhood in the 1950s (New York, 2018; online edn, Oxford Academic, 21 June 2018), https://doi.org/10.1093/oso/9780190675684.003.0006

10. Roos, Dave, "How the Cold War Space Race Led to US Students Doing Tons of Homework." History, August 13, 2019, https://www.history.com/news/homework-cold-war-sputnik

11. "Coming Out From the Shadows: A History of Gay and Lesbian Educators in the United States," California Council on Teacher Education, 2014, https://www.ccte.org/wp-content/pdfs-conferences/ccte-conf-sample-practice-proposal.pdf

12. Graves, Karen, And They Were Wonderful Teachers: Florida's Purge of Gay and Lesbian Teachers. University of Illinois Press, 2009.

13. Austin, Tyler, "Today In Gay History: Gay Activist Pies Anita Bryant In the Face." Out, October 14, 2016, https://www.out.com/today-gay-history/2016/10/14/today-gay-history-gay-activist-pies-anita-bryant-face#toggle-gdpr

14. Endres, Nikolai, "Bryant, Anita (b. 1940)." GLBTQ Archive, 2009, http://www.glbtqarchive.com/ssh/bryant_anita_S.pdf

15. Simbro, William, "Pie Shoved in Anita Bryant's Face by Homosexual Here –She Cries." The Des Moines Register, October 15, 1977, https://www.newspapers.com/article/the-des-moines-register/20071567/

16. Levin, Josh, "Anita Bryant's War on Gay Rights," July 8, 2021, in One Year: 1977, podcast, format audio, 01:04:40, https://slate.com/podcasts/one-year/s1/1977/e1/anita-bryant-gay-rights-1977

17. Eler, Alicia, Chris Hewitt, Rick Nelson and Jenna Ross, "50 Years of Twin Cities Pride," Star Tribune, June 16, 2022, https://www2.startribune.com/50-years-anniversary-twin-cities-gay-pride-parade-minneapolis-st-paul-lesbian-lgbt-lgbtq-history/600180582/?refresh=true.

18. Barabak, Mark, "Column: 'So exhausted'. She helped win an early gay rights fight but now sees the country moving backward," Los Angeles Times, April 6, 2022, https://www.latimes.com/politics/story/2022-04-06/florida-dont-say-gay-law-california-briggs-initiative-harvey-milk

19. Tracey, Liz, "Proposition 6 (The Briggs Initiative): Annotated." JSTOR Daily, October 28, 2022, https://daily.jstor.org/proposition-6-the-briggs-initiative-annotated/

20. Milk, Harvey. "The Hope Speech," transcript of speech delivered at San Francisco City Hall, June 25, 1978, https://terpconnect.umd.edu/~jklumpp/ARD/MilkSpeech.pdf

21. Tracey, "Prop 6."

22. "*Schroer v. Billington*," Cases, ACLU, accessed on July 2, 2024, https://www.acludc.org/en/cases/schroer-v-billington

23. ACLU, "*Schroer v. Billington.*"

24. "Frequently Asked Questions: What the EEOC's Decision in *Macy v. Holder* Means for You," Transgender Law Center, updated May 1, 2012, https://transgenderlawcenter.org/wp-content/uploads/2013/06/92419763-F-A-Q-EEOC-Ruling-in-Mia-Macy-V-Eric-Holder.pdf

25. McCammon, Sarah and Nina Totenberg, "Supreme Court overturns *Roe v. Wade*, ending right to abortion upheld for decades," NPR, June 24, 2022, https://www.npr.org/2022/06/24/1102305878/supreme-court-abortion-roe-v-wade-decision-overturn

26. "Employment Nondiscrimination," Equality Maps, Movement Advancement Project, accessed July 12, 2024, https://www.lgbtmap.org/equality-maps/employment_non_discrimination_laws
27. Baptiste, Nathalie, "In A Deep-Red Florida County, This Gay Teacher Quit To Save Her Career," Huffpost, June 2, 2023, https://www.huffpost.com/entry/florida-teacher-resigns-lgbtq_n_647a19d1e4b0a7554f444ac6
28. Butera, Isabelle, "Accused of Indoctrination, Targeted by the Right: They Just Want to Teach," USA Today, August 12, 2023, https://www.usatoday.com/story/news/education/2023/08/12/a-look-inside-the-classrooms-of-lgbtq-and-allied-teachers-across-the-country/70488782007/

CHAPTER FOUR

Let's Talk Numbers

Finding the Numbers

No matter how compelling the emotional argument might be for providing safe and affirming environments for LGBTQ+ students, some people will never be convinced that it's worth a solid look until it's laid out in the cold hard data. This is certainly true for those of us who have spent our careers navigating academia and the bureaucracy of school systems, where a teacher can't blow their nose without evidence that it's aligned to the Common Core.

Data collection in queer circles, especially for children under 18, can be challenging for several reasons. Historically, it has relied very heavily on self-reporting, which was and still is a dangerous ask in many parts of the country. When the consequences for your neighbors, your classmates, or even your family discovering your sexuality or gender identity can be extremely high, it might not seem worth it for the benefit of a random social scientist's PhD research. More recently, this kind of data collection has become highly politicized, and there are entire universities, state health departments, and school districts that straight refuse to ask their populations anything that feels, and this is not a direct quote, "kinda gay."

Even if there are groups in alignment with the need to collect information related to sexual orientation and gender identity (commonly just called SOGI+), there are now a hundred voices disagreeing about common terminology, definitions, and scope. What should the options be when selecting for gender? Should "lesbian" be an item separate from "gay"? What happens when an old term falls out of fashion and a new one is adopted? The argument continues, and we go another year without knowing who's out there and what they need.

Luckily, there are groups that have managed to cut through the noise to deliver sound information, even if it's more limited than we want. So here it is, an argument in numbers.

The Kids Are All Gay

No one is quite as queer as Gen Z.

Gallup has been collecting SOGI+ data for more than a decade, first asking respondents to give their best approximation of their identities back in 2012. Back then, they found that about 3.5% of the US population identified as LGBTQ+, but that number has jumped to 7.6% overall, with Gen Z self-identifying at a whopping 22.3%. That's in pretty stark contrast to those of us born when *Home Alone* was in theaters (1990); my fellow Millennials are rocking at about 9.8%. In distant last place are Boomers, holding steady at less than 3%.[1]

There are a lot of theories about why this is happening, the least interesting being "TikTok and/or the fluoride in the water is making kids *really* into Chappell Roan." It's more likely that as it's become less dangerous to be openly queer, more of us are willing to risk it all for a life where we feel a little less trapped inside of ourselves. There's an oft-circulated chart[2] showing a similar jump in the number of left-handed Americans after it fell out of fashion for teachers and parents to try to "correct" children into right handedness. Something similar is happening with autism, which is being diagnosed in children at a much higher rate now (about 27.6 in every 1,000) than in the year 2000 (closer to 6.7 in 1,000).[3] There's no cabbage patch full of queer, autistic, left-handed kids that is suddenly being tended to with alarming vigor in the last 20 years – we're just much more likely to raise children in environments that nurture their true and authentic selves. Instead of feeling trapped, alone, and isolated, our kids are seeing their differences as a celebrated and natural part of vibrant human existence.

The more depressing potential contributor to this number asks us to look back into recent queer history. The AIDS epidemic, which raged largely unchecked from 1981 through the 1990s, took more than 100,000 American lives,[4] most of whom were gay and bisexual men. As we took the disease, along with its treatment and prevention, more seriously, the resulting deaths dropped dramatically.

So, we can choose to see the spike in LGBTQ+ kids as alarming if we want, but I don't tend to. We're seeing more of them (and more of them are surviving) than we ever have before.

Checking the Facts Against the Feelings

No matter the underlying reason for the uptick in queer-identifying young adults, the result is that when we're talking about LGBTQ+ student experiences at school, we are capturing what it is like for 1 in 5 American children to attend class in this country every single day.

So, what's it like?

> "When we talk about the experiences of queer kids, we are often looking into rates of suicidality, self-harm, harassment and bullying, and other topics that may be upsetting and/or personally triggering. If it will be a tough or impossible read for you, feel free to skip ahead to the end of the bulleted list. If you're looking for a quick overview, here it is: it's tough to be queer, and it's not getting easier."

The largest scale data we have on this experience comes from GLSEN (formerly called the Gay, Lesbian & Straight Education Network) and the Trevor Project. Both routinely conduct surveys of LGBTQ+ youth (between the ages of 13 and 18) and focus exclusively on their lived experiences. Here's what they've found for these populations recently[5,6,7]:

From GLSEN:

- 73% experienced symptoms of anxiety.
- 58% experienced symptoms of depression.
- 45% considered attempting suicide this year.
- 14% attempted suicide this year.
- While some numbers are trending downward in recent years, anxiety and suicidality are rising.

From *The Trevor Project:

- 68% felt unsafe at school because of their sexual orientation or gender identity.
- 32.2% missed school in the last month because they felt unsafe or uncomfortable.
- 11.3% missed four or more school days in the last month.
- 16.2% changed schools over safety concerns.
- 78.8% avoided school functions or extracurriculars.
- Between 39.4% and 45.1% avoided school bathrooms, locker rooms, and physical education classes.
- LGBTQ+ high school students used substances such as alcohol and marijuana at significantly higher rates than their peers.
- 56% used alcohol in the last year.
- 34% used marijuana in the last year.
- 11% used a prescription drug that was not prescribed to them in the last year.

What is happening here? Why are so many of our kids suffering? Why, in this time where we're seeing a historic rise in self-identification, are we also seeing a ton of kids who would rather self-medicate, skip school, or even end their lives than get on the bus in the morning?

One answer is to assume that there is something inherently damaging about identifying as queer. There are several politicians and anti-LGBTQ+ advocates who have made the claim that a child's psyche and self-worth are fractured the moment they begin questioning their gender or sexuality (but especially their gender). Vivek Ramaswamy, pharmaceutical entrepreneur and one-time presidential hopeful, claimed on a national stage in 2024 that "transgenderism,[i] especially in kids, is a mental health disorder," following up with, "… And I'm sorry, it is not compassionate to affirm a kid's confusion."[8] This mirrors statements made by his colleagues the same year, such as one made on Fox Business Network by Representative Tim Burchett of Tennessee: "It's a mental illness. We just gotta address it. It's… it's not a, it's not a normal type lifestyle."[9]

In Kansas, Representative John Eplee used his credentials as a physician to repeat a similar sentiment during state health committee hearings, arguing that he believes 80–90% of the time, people change their mind about being transgender entirely, and that, in his words, "We're in the middle of what I think is a social contagion right now."[10]

Their feelings are, largely, that to be transgender is to be damaged and that there is little else to do to solve that damage than remove the chance to live an adult life as a trans person.

But this isn't a chapter about feelings. We're here for numbers.

So, what do the numbers say? Are trans people damaged?

In 2022, someone finally asked us. Between October and December, the National Center for Transgender Equality conducted the largest and most comprehensive survey of transgender Americans ever attempted[11]: 92,329 trans people over 16 completed a survey with more than 300 possible questions. It took, on average, more than an hour to

---

[i] "Transgenderism" is a word used primarily within anti-trans rhetoric, as it frames our identities as ideologies or belief systems, which they are not. Don't use it.

complete (and I would know, I took it too). If we were ever going to learn about the long-term destructive effects of "transgenderism,"[ii] it would be now.

But that's not what we found.

Instead, 94% of us said we were more satisfied with our life now than we were pre-transition. 79% of us even said we were "a lot" more satisfied. 98% of us said that hormone treatment improved our lives, almost identically matched by the 97% of us who felt the same about our gender-affirming surgeries.

So, if that's not it – if the dissatisfaction, disaffection, and alienation aren't bubbling up from a place of deep internal misalignment, why is it happening at all?

The Seeds and the Soil

I think in moments like this about my many misadventures in gardening. As a recent desert expat, I really overestimated my abilities when I first set to assembling, tilling, and planting my garden this past spring. My husband and I optimistically purchased a handful of those huge paper bags full of "assorted" seeds when they popped up in seasonal sections at the end of the winter, dreaming of an abundant garden that we could harvest in the summer. I was particularly excited for the possibility of six-foot-tall sunflowers, as I pushed each of them point down into the earth along our front fence. Won't it be nice, I thought, when the whole front of our house is blocked from the road with rows and rows of healthy bright yellow flowers.

What happened instead was, predictably, close to nothing. A few seedlings bravely pushed through the dirt at first but didn't make it very far. Others withered the inch and a half down right where they'd been planted. A thousand seeds and not a single blossom.

My first instinct was to blame the seeds. A thousand of them, and not a single one could bother to grow? What were the odds of that? We'd

---

[ii] Really though, don't use this word.

come out every morning and stood dutifully with the garden hose, soaking the earth down to the clay. We'd looked up how to plant them, how far down, and at what time of year. We checked every box, considered every angle, and it just didn't make sense. I could just *feel* that they should have grown.

But yeah, this isn't a chapter about feelings.

When a seed doesn't grow, we don't blame the seed: we examine the soil. We look at the conditions. We think about the thousand other variables that come into play when it seems just a little ridiculous to assume that a thousand sunflowers plotted against you, and themselves, specifically.

But it wasn't them. I started a new batch (indoors this time), controlling the temperature, and using the good potting soil from a plant shop and not from the gnat-infested mega bags they sold in front of the hardware store. I kept a little plastic lid over them when they were small, protecting them from the dry air that had robbed the first set of all their moisture. The neighborhood birds, who last time swooped in and stole our seeds right from the ground moments after they were planted, were kept at bay. Less than a week later, almost every single plant was thriving.

It turns out that even though I hadn't considered a particular barrier, it still existed, and it had an impact on my seeds.

So, what does the soil look like for queer kids right now?

Over the last few years, the American Civil Liberties Union (ACLU) has been tracking the number of anti-LGBTQ+ bills introduced through state legislatures. They review and log anything proposed within free speech and expression, barriers to accurate IDs, healthcare restrictions, bans on public accommodations (like restrooms and locker rooms), restrictions on the rights of students and educators, the weakening of civil rights protections, bans on marriage equality, and anything that preempts local nondiscrimination protections, across all 50 states.

As of December 2024, the last time the tracker was updated, that tally was at 574.[12] At the same time in 2023, the number was 469.

As queer lives become more overtly politicized, the hate, vitriol, and negativity are leaching into the earth where we're trying to grow healthy queer kids.

In another poll by the Trevor Project conducted in 2023, this story is supported by the numbers: 86% of transgender and nonbinary youth reported that debates around anti-trans bills negatively impacted their mental health, while 45% of trans youth experienced cyberbullying for the same reason.[13] Additionally, 75% of LGBTQ+ young people reported that threats of violence against LGBTQ+ community centers, pride events, drag shows, or transgender health clinics raised their stress and anxiety levels.

Because so many of these policies inevitably surround their experiences at school, those apprehensions manifest across the board when we look at more specific attacks on trans and nonbinary students. In the case of "forced outing" policies, where school staff are compelled to tell a student's family if they see or hear of them using a different name or pronouns, 67% of transgender and nonbinary youth report feeling angry, 54% felt stressed, and 51% felt fear. Anger is the most prominent feeling for policies that ban teachers from discussing LGBTQ+ topics in the classroom and eliminate LGBTQ+ books in school libraries, at 66% for queer kids overall, and 80% for those who are transgender and nonbinary.[14]

The Data Behind the Schoolhouse Door

Pulling the lens in a little bit, it's worth wondering if all the national hubbub is still too distant to have a real impact on the day-to-day well-being of LGBTQ+ students. After all, most of the egregious anti-queer (and again, more specifically anti-trans) legislation and policy is occurring in just a handful of states. And while that makes life especially challenging for kids living in places like Texas and Idaho,[iii] there's always the

---

[iii] There are currently 26 states and 3 US territories rates "low" or "very low" in the Movement Advancement Project's rankings of LGBTQ+ equality protections.

option to move to one of the 21 states with stronger LGBTQ+ protections. Certainly, children in these areas are shielded from the worst of it.

Once again, that doesn't track with the numbers.

In the same GLAAD report that found high levels of anxiety, depression, and suicidality in LGBTQ+ youth across the country, nearly all surveyed students (at 97%) heard "gay" used in a derogatory way during the school day. In addition, 89.9% heard other homophobic remarks, 91.8% heard negative comments about gender expression, and 83.4% heard disparaging comments made specifically against transgender people.

And it carried over to the adults in their lives too.

Fifty-eight percent of students reported hearing explicitly homophobic comments from their teachers or other school staff, and only one in ten reported seeing school staff intervene "most of the time" during incidents of anti-LGBTQ+ derogatory remarks.[15]

There are several surveys and data sets that dive into the experiences LGBTQ+ kids endure related to bullying, harassment, and violence at school, but I always come back to one in particular, as it hits very close to home for me, because I taught at a school in one of the "safest" possible states in the union. California has an ironclad number of protections, especially within schools, but policies don't always reach from the statehouse to the reality of the classroom. In 2016, a study was conducted out of Chapman University, less than 30 miles from where I was teaching. It pulled data from the California Healthy Kids Survey, comparing answers related to school climate and student mental health from every county in the state, and made the results available to the public. The comparisons told us that universally, even in one of the most protected states in the country, LGBTQ+ students were suffering (see Figure 4.1).[16]

There is no opting out of the shared reality experienced by queer kids across the country. The data tells us that no matter who is asking or where they're asking it, the answer is the same: it really sucks to be LGBTQ+, but not because of us.

	LGB	Non-LGB	Trans	Non-Trans
	5.4%	94.6%	1.0%	99.0%
Attendance				
How many times did you skip school or cut class in the past 12 months? (more than once a week)	5.1%	1.9%	7.1%	2.1%
Missed school because you felt very, sad, hopeless, anxious, stressed, angry? (past 30 days)	25.1%	6.9%	23.1%	7.7%
Missed school because you didn't feel safe at school? (past 30 days)	4.1%	1.1%	8.8%	1.2%
Safety				
How safe do you feel when you are at school? (unsafe or very unsafe)	10.3%	4.1%	21.2%	4.3%
Have you been in a physical fight? (past 12 months)	15.6%	9.0%	24.0%	9.3%
Have you carried a gun at school? (past 12 months)	3.3%	1.1%	10.8%	1.2%
Did you ever seriously consider attempting suicide? (past 12 months)	45.8%	13.5%	49.2%	15.2%
Did you ever feel so sad or hopeless almost everyday for two weeks or more that you stopped doing some usual activities? (past 12 months)	61.5%	24.9%	51.8%	26.6%

	LGB	Non-LGB	Trans	Non-Trans
Bullying and harassment				
In the past 12 months on school property have you...				
• Been pushed, shoved, slapped, hit, kicked by someone 1 or more times	29.5%	19.1%	36.3%	19.5%
• Been afraid of being beaten up?	22.9%	11.4%	32.2%	11.9%
• Had rumors/lies spread about you?	48.7%	30.3%	50.2%	31.1%
• Had sexual jokes, comments, or gestures made to you?	53.0%	26.9%	52.6%	28.1%
• Been made fun of because of your looks or way you talked?	49.9%	28.0%	51.5%	28.9%
• Been threatened with harm or injury?	17.3%	7.6%	25.2%	8.0%
• Been made fun of, insulted, or called names?	53.5%	33.0%	53.4%	33.9%
• Been threatened or injured with a weapon (gun, knife, club, etc.)?	7.4%	2.8%	17.2%	3.0%
• Have other students spread mean rumors or lies about you on the Internet?	30.6%	17.8%	33.7%	18.4%
• Were harassed or bullied for your race, ethnicity, or national origin?	22.0%	12.9%	30.5%	13.2%
• Were harassed or bullied for your religion?	12.2%	6.6%	18.5%	6.8%
• Were harassed or bullied for your gender?	23.5%	5.9%	35.4%	6.6%
• Were harassed or bullied because you are gay or lesbian or somebody thought you were?	43.2%	5.0%	42.4%	6.7%
• Were harassed or bullied because physical or mental disability?	12.4%	2.9%	20.8%	3.3%
• Were harassed or bullied for any other reason?	32.7%	15.6%	36.6%	16.3%

FIGURE 4.1 California Healthy Kids Survey 2016

But…But…the Children!

Ideally, the laws and policies that we write to safeguard America's youth should be backed by data and supported by evidence. Children are vulnerable, their brains are still ever-growing sponges, and as a nonvoting demographic, they rely on those of us with agency to stand up for them when we know they're facing an external and preventable danger.

Is any of the noise around anti-LGBTQ+ sentiment really about protecting children?

Proponents still seem to think so, arguing that kids are not only impressionable and often scarred when they are exposed to potentially traumatizing experiences but also facing physical consequences of which they can't possibly understand the consequences. Even if the numbers are small, any chance for trauma and regret is too large to be ignored.

Let's check the numbers again.

If we say we're concerned about protecting the innocence and appropriate cognitive development of America's youth, that's in direct contrast to many recently rolled back child labor protections we're seeing in a few US states.

Iowa, for example, allows children as young as 14 work in meat coolers and industrial laundries and only holds an age minimum of 15 for children to work on assembly lines around dangerous machinery.

In Arkansas, work permits that tracked a young person's proof of age, their working hours, and written consent of a parent or guardian for children as young as 14 have been scrapped entirely.[17]

If we say we're worried about the potential for damage to children's physical bodies, there are several statistics that seem like immediate cause for concern and action.

As of September 2024, corporal punishment, or the practice of disciplining students with physical violence such as paddling or spanking, is legal in 17 US states and actively practiced in 14.[18] During the 2017–2018 school year, roughly 69,000 students were on the receiving end of this violence.[19]

Outside of the classroom, body traumas and even fatalities are reported in shocking yearly frequency as a result of youth contact sports, with football at the top of the list with total injuries (at 110,171 reported in children ages 5–14 in 2021) and rates of concussions (10.4 concussions per 10,000 athlete exposures).[20] In 2023, 16 children died playing football, with three of those deaths due to traumatic injuries on the field.[21]

If we say we're worried about children making life-altering and adult decisions, potentially even under duress, we might want to sound the alarm.

Only 13 US states hold a firm minimum age for marriage at 18.[22] With no federally established minimum, between 2000 and 2018, nearly 300,000 children have been married in the United States, with a vast majority of those being girls wed to much older men.[23]

And while there are 23 states that have banned "conversion therapy," the abusive practice of attempting to change the sexual orientation or gender identity of a minor through damaging and pseudoscientific means, there are still more than 1,320 conversion therapy practitioners operating in the United States today.[24]

Holistically, the leading causes of death among children and young adults in the United States, in ascending order, are heart disease, drowning, drug overdose, car accidents, and firearms.[25]

And while some of these problems are treated with the same vigor and urgency as pronouns and LGBTQ+ libraries, quite a few are not. So, after reviewing the data, absent entirely of our feelings, we have to wonder: What would our country look like if we prioritized the real dangers our children are facing? Where would we focus our time? Our money? What could we be capable of changing if we looked past our assumptions and agreed that our kids deserve more from us?

Notes

1. Jones, Jeffrey, "LGBTQ+ Identification in U.S. Now at 7.6%," Gallup, March 13, 2024, https://news.gallup.com/poll/611864/lgbtq-identification.aspx
2. Ingraham, Christopher, "The Surprising Geography of American Left-Handedness," The Washington Post, September 22, 2015, https://www.washingtonpost.com/news/wonk/wp/2015/09/22/the-surprising-geography-of-american-left-handedness/
3. Richter, Felix, "The Rising Prevalence of Autism," Statista, April 2, 2024, https://www.statista.com/chart/29630/identified-prevalence-of-autism-spectrum-disorder-in-the-us/

4. "Snapshots of an Epidemic: An HIV/AIDS Timeline," The Foundation for AIDS Research, accessed April 30, 2024, https://www.amfar.org/about-hiv-aids/snapshots-of-an-epidemic-hiv-aids/

5. "2022 National Survey on LGBTQ Youth Mental Health," The Trevor Project, accessed May 1, 2024, https://www.thetrevorproject.org/survey-2022/

6. "The 2021 National School Climate Survey," GLSEN, accessed May 1, 2024, https://www.glsen.org/research/2021-national-school-climate-survey

7. "Substance Use and Suicide Risk Among LGBTQ Youth," 2021 National Survey on LGBTQ Youth Mental Health, The Trevor Project, accessed May 1, 2024, https://www.thetrevorproject.org/research-briefs/substance-use-and-suicide-risk-among-lgbtq-youth-jan-2022/

8. "Election 2024: Candidates Ignore LGBTQ Issues in the Second GOP Primary Debate," Elections, GLAAD, September 28, 2023, https://glaad.org/election2024-simi-valley-gop-debate/

9. Fitzpatrick, John, "Fox Host Shuts Down Republican's Transgender Comment," Newsweek, April 2, 2024, https://www.newsweek.com/tim-burchett-transgender-mental-illness-maria-bartiromo-1885911.

10. Smith, Sherman, "Kansas Democrats blast GOP physicians for pushing disinformation in debate on anti-trans bill," Kansas Reflector, March 7, 2024, https://kansasreflector.com/2024/03/07/kansas-democrats-blast-gop-physicians-for-pushing-disinformation-in-debate-on-anti-trans-bill/

11. Durso, Heng-Lehtinen, Herman and James, "Trans Survey."

12. "Mapping Attacks on LGBTQ Rights in U.S. State Legislatures in 2024," LGBTQ Rights, ACLU, last updated on December 6, 2024, https://www.aclu.org/legislative-attacks-on-lgbtq-rights-2024

13. "New Poll Emphasizes Negative Impacts of Anti-LGBTQ Policies on LGBTQ Youth," Press, The Trevor Project, January 19, 2023, https://www.thetrevorproject.org/blog/new-poll-emphasizes-negative-impacts-of-anti-lgbtq-policies-on-lgbtq-youth/

14. Tabachnick, Cara, "Mental health of LGBTQ youth worsening in current 'hostile political climate', survey finds," CBS News, May 1, 2023, https://www.cbsnews.com/news/trevor-project-mental-health-lgbtq-youth-worsening-in-hostile-political-climate/

15. GLSEN, "2021 Climate Survey."

16. California Healthy Kids Survey Data 2016. Data Analysis Prepared by Kris DePedro, PhD and John Elfers, PhD. ACLU of California and Chapman University.

17. Fliter, John and Betsy Wood, "States are Weakening their Child Labor Restrictions Nearly 8 Decades after the US Government Took Kids out of the Workforce," The Conversation, June 26, 2023, https://theconversation.com/states-are-weakening-their-child-labor-restrictions-nearly-8-decades-after-the-us-government-took-kids-out-of-the-workforce-205175.

18. The practice is both legal and practiced in Alabama, Arkansas, Florida, Georgia, Indiana, Kentucky, Louisiana, Mississippi, Missouri, North Carolina, Oklahoma, South Carolina, Tennessee, and Texas. In Wyoming, Kansas, and Arizona, corporal punishment is legal, but there are no reported institutions actively practicing it.

19. Greene-Santos, Aniya, "Corporal Punishment in Schools Still Legal in Many States," NEA Today, May 20, 2024, https://www.nea.org/nea-today/all-news-articles/corporal-punishment-schools-still-legal-many-states#:~:text=As%20of%202024%2C%20corporal%20punishment,In%20May%202023%2C%20Sen.

20. Holcombe, Madeline, "3 Kids have Tragically Died of Football Injuries this Year. Experts help Weigh Pros and Cons of Sports," CNN, August 30, 2024, https://www.cnn.com/2024/08/30/health/sports-injury-kids-safety-wellness/index.html

21. Jacoby, Sarah, "13-Year-Old Football Player Died During Practice. He's Part of a National Trend," Today, August 29, 2024, https://www.today.com/health/news/youth-football-deaths-rcna168779

22. "Child Marriage in the United States," Equality Now, last modified on June 17, 2024, https://equalitynow.org/learn_more_child_marriage_us/

23. "Legislation to End Child Marriage in the U.S." Unchained At Last, accessed on June 2, 2024, https://www.unchainedatlast.org/laws-to-end-child-marriage/

24. "It's Still Happening: A Report on Practitioners of So-Called Conversation 'Therapy' in the U.S." The Trevor Project, 2023, https://www.thetrevorproject.org/wp-content/uploads/2023/12/FINAL_Its-Still-Happening-Report.pdf

25. Carter, Patrick, Rebecca Cunningham and Jason Goldstick, "Current Causes of Death in Children and Adolescents in the United States," The New England Journal of Medicine 386, no. 20 (2022) 1955–1956, https://www.nejm.org/doi/full/10.1056/NEJMc2201761

PART
II

Get Your Mind Right

CHAPTER FIVE

But What Can I Do on Monday?

There's this moment in *The Great Gatsby* where a party guest is pulling big fancy leather tomes down from shelves in the titular host's massive library. He says to Nick Carraway, the novel's narrator, that Gatsby "didn't cut the pages," as he opens each one and tosses it aside for the next. It's one of my favorite moments to explain to students, because it's got a bit of 1920s trivia hidden inside of it – before the second half of the twentieth century, publishers would print entire books onto one long page and then fold and glue it into the binding. It was up to the reader to take a knife to each fold and slice it open, a laborious enough task that it's only something you would do if you were really dedicated to reading. Ultimately, the guest is bringing it up because it's obvious that Gatsby hasn't read any of the hundreds of books in his own collection; the whole spread is just a showpiece for appearances.

While we may be saved the embarrassment of uncut pages now, there are a lot of teachers and administrators who, I am sure, have whole shelves behind their desks stacked with professional development books that have suspiciously creaseless spines.

There's no shame in it, really. I'm guilty too. It seems to me that throughout the decade I spent inside of public schools, I couldn't escape an in-service day, curricular seminar, or teaching conference without a stack of new paperbacks written by former principals and education PhDs, all with very impressive résumés and mouths full of exceptionally white teeth. While there were several of these books that positively informed my practice as a teacher, there were even more that felt like a waste of shelf space from the beginning. They collected dust in my room for years, because they didn't answer the one question those of us in the trenches always end up asking:

"Okay, but what can I do on Monday?"

Teachers are short on time and energy, and we always appreciate cutting right to the point. Like, let's skip the story about how you used to make these brownies with your grandma – just jump to the recipe, please and thank you.

And this is fair. When professional development is crowded with theory and short on practical, immediately applicable strategies, I have struggled to see the value, and I am immediately suspicious of the author. During my time in the classroom, I got fed up with vague language and generalized advice that wasn't followed up with how any of it could be realistically applied to what I was doing with my students, and that's exactly the reason why there were quite a few promising titles gifted or donated to me that never saw daylight after I passed the table of contents.

There are an alarming number of centralized values like this in professional development for educators that are always paired with nebulous instructions. If you want me to promote "resilience and grit" in my classroom, what does that look like? How do you want me to do it, specifically? How will you know when you walk in on my students during the school day that they are especially gritty? I still don't know.

If we say we want campuses and classrooms that promote inclusion, acceptance, and equity, it is a disservice to not also answer *HOW* that should (or could) look. Talking in circles about how important something is without offering pragmatic solutions and next steps would be unhelpful and infuriating.

I promise you now that I won't do that...

...but

You kind of have to meet me halfway here.

If I promise not to drown you in theory and to offer real, valuable, and tangible lessons, frames, templates, and advice, you have to promise me some things too:

Don't skip the stuff between now and then.

Don't jump over the stories, the intros, and the explanations.

Don't wave away the parts that ask you to participate in real self-reflection. Don't flip past the heavy bits.

Because without doing the harder work, the part that asks us to establish a new kind of mindset together, everything afterward is as good as garbage – *really*. All of it loses its potency, withers and rots to nothing, becomes effectively useless the moment it is used without a grounding in why and how we're doing it. It's true even if you have a ton of experience, it's true even if you've already been doing this kind of work for a long time, and it's true even if you are a part of this community too.

Here's an example.

One of my first jobs after I left teaching was with a cancer nonprofit, where I trained doctors and other health professionals about the specific disparities faced by trans people who undergo cancer diagnosis and treatment. I was often in rooms with exceptionally educated people who had entire alphabets of degrees after their names, and I was responsible for telling them that, even if they were doing their best, they were likely doing at least a handful of things that were harmful to their queer patients. In short, I was not always well received.

By far, the most popular question at every single training was the healthcare version of "Okay, but what can we do on Monday?" Everyone, from receptionists to medical directors, wanted to know what secret, easy, frictionless strategy would transform their hospital into a welcoming queer utopia. I would review websites, healthcare plans, waiting room layouts, and patient intake forms; write up a list of recommendations; and inevitably get the same response. After a quick review of my feedback, I would hear, "This is a lot. What if instead we put pronouns on our name tags? Would that help?"

In one particularly heated exchange, I got an email from a physician who was a highly respected oncologist in a decorated hospital. Upset about a suggestion, she typed up a very detailed and shockingly transphobic response. It was vile, presumptuous, rude, condescending, and nestled right above an email signature that listed her pronouns as "she/her/hers" in a swoopy and delicate font.

Essentially, yes, there are simple changes, easy shifts, and updated language that will help us to create a more welcoming environment for queer people, but without the rest of the work, at best they are empty gestures and at worst actively harmful bait-and-switches. Memorizing a glossary, sticking pronouns in an email signature – these are steps that are helpful but only at the very surface. Like cutting a weed instead of pulling it, there's likely more work to do deeper in the soil.

CHAPTER SIX

Taking Inventory

If You're Asking, You Know

If there's any twenty-first-century queer experience that is likely universal, it's this:

At some point, almost every single one of us has opened a private browser tab to search "Am I Gay?"...as if a single search engine has the insight to answer a question like that. Hilariously, the answer is in the question. Straight people don't spend a lot of time combing through quizzes and search results to confirm their sexual orientation. If you spend a lot of time wondering if you might be gay, you probably are.

This is true also when you ask yourself, "Am I doing enough to show my students I care? Do they know that I'm trying? That I want to learn and grow for them?"

If you're asking, you already have the answer.

Intentions and attitude are most of the battle within allyship, and most people who have already chosen a career rooted in service are in great shape. And there's always room to improve, and we may take a wrong turn. However, the critical issue here is that most of the people who are doing the most harm to queer kids have zero idea, and they don't care. They aren't wringing their hands worried that they might do or say the wrong thing, and they aren't picking up and thumbing through books like this hoping to course correct. Those of us who are asking "How can I do better?" are not the ones who opened the wound, but we are the ones who are doing our best to stop the bleeding. We might not be amazing at it yet, but we're still doing our very best. So, before we do some reflection together, take one of those mighty healing breaths deep into your lungs, hold it for just a couple of seconds, and let it all out, because *you are doing great*.

What Are You Already Doing?

Reflecting on the current practices in our classrooms is a critical first step when we're evaluating where we need to begin, and most of these evaluations have absolutely nothing to do with queer identity or visibility. Most of the practices that make your classroom better for queer kids have nothing to do with books and pronouns, so this reflection is less about checking off how many rainbow flags are crammed into that coffee mug full of pens on your desk and more about considering your daily interactions with students. Because as much as we hope that our very carefully planned lessons will stick with them forever and ever, most of what they pick up from us is what we model for them – our routines, behaviors, actions, and reactions.

For your queer students, they're going to take in and use anything they learn from observing you to determine if it's safe to exist authentically in your classroom and whether you can be trusted when they feel unsafe from issues of violence, bullying, and harassment to smaller discomforts they might not even know how to name. For the rest of your students, you're one of many adults modeling for them how to show up in the world as an LGBTQ+ ally, and they won't know what you don't show them. While it might be uncomfortable to be clear where you stand, any compassion and respect you model now has the potential to ripple out into a world way beyond your current horizon.

Use these questions as a starting point in your own reflective process and remember discomfort is a good sign. Like a hermit crab outgrowing our shells, it's always going to feel a little snug when we're ready to grow:

- **What does failure look like? For them and for you?**

    Failure is inevitable, especially when we're trying something for the first time. For our students, most of what they are doing they are doing for the first time. They're trying out their weird wobbly giraffe legs on solid ground right before our eyes, and it's highly likely that they're going to stumble in front of us. What does that look like for them? How much room is there for them to fail and try again? This isn't just about academics either. They don't know how to ask for help, how to write a polite email, how to apologize when their emotions take over and they trip over their words, or how to back down when they're embarrassed in front of their friends. When failure is normalized and treated with patience, they learn that all hope is not lost forever when they don't get it right away. As adults, because our lives are busy and we're on year 10 of seeing the same fumble repeatedly, it can be exceptionally challenging to remember that our frustration isn't helpful and that our lack of patience with them is often a projection. Because here are the harder questions: How often do your students see *you* fail? Do you own your mistakes? Do you show them what it looks like to recognize that something didn't work and how to try again?

    This is helpful because…allyship is all about growing and pivoting. Unhelpful allies will often center their own feelings when they realize they've made a wrong turn, and it's largely because they don't know what to do with the shame that comes with failure.

- **How do you model grace and resilience?**

    This one goes hand in hand with failure but deserves its own reflection. When something isn't working or you realize you've made a mistake, what does it look like for you to bounce back? Again, this is specifically resilience that you model for your students. Do they see you obsess and spiral? Do you suppress how you're feeling so they never see you vulnerable? Do you snap and project that shame back onto them? This isn't a question meant to add to any guilt we're carrying around about how our feelings show up in the classroom, but it can help to expose where we have room for authentic processing. If we encourage our students to take chances and recover quickly when their plans don't pan out the way they expected, we have to model what that looks like.

*This is helpful because...*vulnerability is scary, but it's the only way we're able to see and connect with one another. Your students need to see that not only is it okay to fail, but there is also a path back to an emotionally balanced center. When that's not possible, talking through and being open about your process can make it that much easier for them to have grace for themselves and each other when they are discouraged and dysregulated.

- **How hard are you on yourself?**

    When we say kids are always watching, that means *always*. They hear conversations between teachers in between classes, they hear negative self-talk in the hallway, and they see how you look at yourself when you pass a mirror. What are they noticing? This doesn't mean "be perfect all the time" (in fact, that's the opposite of helpful), but try to see yourself through their eyes. Do they see someone who values themselves? Do they see someone who believes they have inherent worth? Or are they watching as you refuse to call in sick for the third day in a row, as you take on two more unpaid extracurriculars and haul work home every weekend even as it wears on you? Do they see an adult who feels at home in their own skin? Or are they watching as you comment on your weight, your height, your clothes, your hairline?

    *This is helpful because...*we're only capable of the same amount of compassion for other people that we have for ourselves. If we believe we're doing our best and that we are worthy and whole without any conditions, it creates the capacity for us to believe that about those around us. To quote Ru Paul, "If you can't love yourself, how the hell are you gonna love somebody else?"

- **In your classroom, how easy is it to change your mind?**

    As frustrating as it is to watch a student march up to your desk to ask if they can change their position on their research topic for the third time, that process is central to the development of a flexible brain. Of all the internal logical fallacies that have done the most harm across history, the "anchor bias" has to be up near the top. This is where, as humans with inflexible natures, we are likely to believe the first perspective we hear, and then die on the hill defending it. Changing our mind can be deeply uncomfortable, because we are still hanging on to the belief that pivoting to a new perspective says something about our character. It does, but not in the way many of us were raised to believe. What it says about us is that we can respond to new information with a new point of view, which is a good thing.

    This is helpful because... a rigid worldview is a disservice to queer people and our allies. From a queer perspective, we are very rarely 100% correct about our own identities right out of the gate. It takes some internal exploration to find terms that work to describe our experiences, and it has to be okay to jump around. *There's no timeline for self-discovery.* And for our allies, it needs to be easier to adapt to new information. Ideally, if someone they care about has a new name? New identity? New pronouns? No problem!

- **Do you ever apologize to your students? What does it look like?**

    Generally, no one apologizes to kids. This is changing a little bit at a time, especially in parenting circles, but it's largely absent from educator training, and I almost never saw it in practice in my time in the classroom. Inevitably, we are going to mess up, and apologizing is an art that we were never taught, *especially* apologizing to children. When you apologize to your students, is it happening publicly? Are you acknowledging the hurt or discomfort that you might have caused? Are you being specific about what you did and why it might have been harmful? When you do apologize, do you center your own feelings and need for forgiveness over theirs?

This is helpful because...existing as a queer person today is traumatic, and we often find ourselves guiding well-meaning allies through the process of apologizing. When handled clumsily, it means that we're pulling double duty: weathering the blow of being treated poorly and then holding emotional space for the feelings of whoever it is who hurt us in the first place. Modeling how to apologize, and when it is appropriate to do so, earns you a front of the line pass at the pearly gates.

- **Where do students see differences and how are differences treated?**

   Today, it is becoming harder to talk about queer life, especially trans life, in the classroom. Restrictive laws and unfriendly climates have all but vanished our existence from K–12 classrooms in a lot of areas across the country, but modeling allyship is still possible in these places. Differences exist in a thousand different ways, and they are all interconnected. How else do they show up in your classroom, in both your curriculum and your student population? What is the racial and ethnic makeup of your school? Is there any kind of spoken or unspoken segregation between accelerated and general ed. classes or where students hang out during lunch and breaks? How do divides of money and class, disability, or neurodivergence factor in? How accessible are extracurriculars, sports, and clubs within these populations?

   This is helpful because...queerness doesn't often exist as an identity in isolation, and modeling conversations (especially uncomfortable ones) about any and all other kinds of inequities can normalize how students will react to and treat each other moving forward, even if they never have a single conversation about LGBTQ+ identity while they are in school.

- **How do you handle and treat IEPs,[i] 504s,[ii] etc.?**

    Yes, it is frustrating trying to run an already under-resourced classroom while juggling a stack of accommodations that push you right up to the edge of your capacity, but think about how you track, respond to, and follow through on those accommodations. Is the language you use around them suggesting that the students who need support are burdens? Do you try to find reasons to work without the accommodations? Do you suspect that many students who have them don't need them? Are you more likely to take recommendations for students with physical disabilities more seriously than students with conditions like dyslexia, autism, ADHD, or anxiety?

    *This is helpful because...*while there is a strong link that suggests LGBTQ+ students have a higher likelihood of being neurodivergent,[1] that isn't really the point here. Classroom accommodations are a good marker for how you feel about changing or pivoting for any of your students' unique needs. This is one way to gauge how open you are to flexibility even when it might be inconvenient or when the reasons for it might not be immediately obvious.

---

[i] An individualized education program (IEP) is a support plan that may include instructional accommodations or guidance to help with the academic and/or social success of a student with a disability.

[ii] A student support plan whose name comes from Section 504 of the Rehabilitation Act of 1973, which prohibits discrimination against people with disabilities in programs that receive federal funding. Unlike an IEP, the plan won't include instruction accommodations and might not be updated as frequently.

- **What campus resources exist for students?**

    Does your campus have a queer student group? Where do they meet? How often? What are the club meetings like? Can staff members drop in and listen? Can students meet with counselors during the day? Do they receive any kind of allyship training? How often? How long do students usually have to wait to see them? What experiences have queer students had with them in the past? Is the nurse on campus trained in LGBTQ+ allyship? The front office staff? Attendance? Custodians? Supervisors? Resource officers? Think about all the adults your students interact with daily: what modeling are they getting from them?

    *This is helpful because...*we see students for only a small fraction of the day, and the more we're able to lean on and support each other, the longer we are all able to carry the load. Getting a more complete picture of your campus climate will help you determine where to focus your energy. Ideally, you aren't in this on your own.

- **What community resources exist for students?**

    Does your city, town, or county have an LGBTQ+ Center? Where is the closest one to your campus? Do they have youth support groups or free counseling? Do they have resources for parents and families? Outside of queer identity-focused groups, what are your students' options for socializing with each other after school? Are most of their options affiliated with religions? Are there any book, game, or coffee shops that host crafting clubs, writers' groups, or tabletop nights? Imagine that you're a young person looking for community in your neighborhood – where can you go?

    *This is helpful because...*if your school doesn't have the kind of supportive community you would want for a young queer person looking for connection, that doesn't mean it doesn't exist. You can always post flyers or host guests from the community at large who might be able to offer alternatives that can make life a smidge easier for LGBTQ+ kids.

- **What does a "run-through" for a queer student look like in your classroom?**

    It's time for some role-playing! Fun! Try to put yourself in the position of a queer student making their way through the school day, week, or year. It can be helpful to try this a couple of times with different intersecting identities. How might a trans tenth grader with ADHD be affected daily in your classroom? Put yourself in their shoes. Walk all the way through what their experience might be, from drop-off to pick up. Consider how close your classroom is to the bathroom. Where would they feel safe sitting? Who will they talk to? What do they have to remember, and how might it be harder to ask for what they need? While you won't know everything, it can be a great place to begin.

    *This is helpful because...*we don't know what we don't know, and we can get stuck inside our own perspective when we don't practice stepping out of it. You can't anticipate or fix every problem area you find, but it will be a lot easier to access empathy when it inevitably surfaces during the year.

The Rainbow-Washed Classroom

Every June, there's a phenomenon that plagues the corporate world in the name of "allyship," and LGBTQ+ activists and advocates have been sounding the alarm about it for years. We call it "rainbow washing": the practice of saturating logos, displays, retail spaces, and digital marketing with as much Pride imagery as possible to cash in on the season and reach into the ever-deepening pockets of queer people and our allies.

On the surface, it doesn't seem particularly insidious. Isn't increased visibility the point? Shouldn't we be happy to see ourselves represented and marketed to after so many years of being ignored entirely? Isn't the front row better than the sidelines?

Not particularly, no.

Plainly, visibility is not safety, and over the last few years, companies that had once been first in line to swap their Instagram logo out for a rainbow doppelganger and sell "Y'all Means All" T-shirts have also been the first to drop the ball when their allyship faced any kind of larger backlash. One by one, groups like Target, Nike, Tractor Supply, Lowe's, and Toyota have scaled back or eliminated their Pride collections and done the same to their diversity, equity, and inclusion programs in the face of increased anti-LGBTQ+ sentiment across the country.[2,3]

Not all efforts for queer visibility are rainbow washing, but all rainbow washers have the same pattern: they put a lot more effort into looking like good allies than doing the work to be those allies. Their attempts lack consideration or input from the community, rarely benefit LGBTQ+ artists and workers, and snap like balsa wood the second they face any pushback from the bigots who stand against them.

And though the phrase "rainbow washing" was never intended for discussions about allyship in education, it still has a place there, even if the intentions are often very different. Because even though many educators want to do their best to show up for the queer students in their care, we still sometimes miss the mark, and the consequences can be very high. An ally who hasn't done their research and committed to some real reckoning with their own knowledge gaps and limitations can sometimes do just as much damage as someone trying to harm us intentionally.

There was a student group on my campus called "We All Belong"[iii] that operated with two well-meaning faculty advisors for many years. Their primary goal was to increase empathy and understanding for all marginalized groups within our school, and they did a pretty good job overall, but I could always feel my heart rate go up as we got closer to their yearly "Week of Caring."[iv] This was because I knew how overworked the

---

[iii] Not the real name.

[iv] Also, not the real name.

staff advisors were and how little of their attention went to supervising the students who took the lead on planning and executing each of the events that would happen throughout the week. One of the days was always specific to LGBTQ+ issues and featured a lunchtime speaker or student panel. I had weird experiences at these events. One year the speaker was a pastor who was not queer but spent her time telling our students that if they were, she would be willing to overlook it and love them anyway. But the last year I attended was absolutely the worst.

The "Week of Caring" that year would, on paper, look like the most successful one yet. This was because our staff of more than 100 teachers would be convinced by the We All Belong faculty advisors to offer their students extra credit for attending one or more of the lunchtime speaking events. This meant the relatively small student crowds we'd seen in the past (at max, 20–30 teenagers in a conference room) ballooned to a borderline unmanageable number of more than a thousand, moving the event to the school's massive theater.

The LGBTQ+ lunchtime event was slated for Thursday, and I watched, horrified, as the crowds only grew from Monday to Wednesday. Students learned that they just had to show up and sit for 20 minutes as they ate their lunch and scrolled TikTok to score an easy five points for exactly no effort. While I loved my time teaching at my school, I was always aware of the kind of student population we hosted. Though the number of homophobic and transphobic incidents in my classroom were low, they weren't zero, and many of my queer students faced routine harassment and bullying from their peers. We didn't live in a particularly progressive part of our county, and teenagers can be cruel no matter who their parents vote for. A crowd this large provided relative anonymity, which is a dangerous combination for an already disengaged audience of adolescents.

My fears were confirmed Thursday afternoon when a handful of student volunteers took the stage and attempted to lecture their peers about the importance of pronouns. There weren't nearly enough stern adults scattered throughout the ocean of students, and a chorus of whispers, chatter, giggles, and jeers rippled through the agonizing 20-minute talk. No one had heard any of what the speakers had tried to say, a thousand 15-year-olds earned extra credit for mocking their queer classmates, and I cried by myself in a hallway during my prep period.

Though no one addressed it when it happened, extra credit wasn't offered the following year.

Incidents like this shouldn't dissuade you from finding opportunities to highlight and uplift queer topics and voices on your own campus, but there's a lesson in here for any teachers who want to avoid rainbow washing in their own classrooms:

1. Listen to and include queer students and adults at every step.
2. Consider how your plan may positively or negatively affect students.
3. Don't bend or deflect when you face likely opposition.

Good intentions mixed with poor planning and bad execution can be a recipe for trauma, both for queer students and for staff. Proceed with caution.

Rainbow washing is one of the most common ally pitfalls, so ask yourself these questions and evaluate how you might react and respond:

- How emotionally safe is your school environment?
- How emotionally safe is your classroom environment?
- How would it feel to hear that you might have accidentally harmed someone?
- How easy is it for you to consider that you may have made a misstep?
- How can your students or colleagues provide you with feedback?
- Are you able to hear that your allyship might still need work?

Grant Me the Grace to Accept the Things I Cannot Change

As much time as we spend with our students, we are still only one small part of their world. By the time a child walks across that stage at their high school graduation, they've sat in more than 40 or 50 classrooms, with at least that many teachers, and interacted with countless administrators, counselors, nurses, classroom aides, bus drivers, supervisors, cafeteria workers, custodians, and coaches. As they get older, our time in their life gets smaller and smaller, receding into the rearview mirror just as quickly as they arrived in ours. And before they get to us, they have already formed perspectives and worldviews shaped by parents, friends, their community, their church, and their social media feed. While our role is an important one and we should do what we can with our time, we also have to see our moment with them as what it is: a blip. Ideally it's a nurturing blip, but it's a blip all the same.

We can't control anything that happens before or after our blip, which can be a challenging reality to live within when you have given so much of yourself to the love that makes good teaching possible. All of us have had to reckon with brilliant and capable students who don't have the resources to go to college, kind and empathetic students who are being ignored and mistreated at home, or passionate students who fall into self-destructive habits that steer them away from a future where we know they might have the potential to thrive. There is so much we can't control, and we can lose ourselves trying to fix it all.

But we can't. We can't fix it all. Teachers tend to abandon ourselves in that effort, and it fully works against us. Even the best, most passionate teachers burnout. In fact, a lot of them do. And it's baked into the profession. It's a feature, not a bug. Consider the rhetoric around teaching; the messaging that we hear from the beginning is

It's about the outcome, not the income.

Don't forget to find your "why."

A good teacher is like a candle – it consumes itself to light the way for others.

I'm sorry, but that's demented. No wonder about 44% of teachers leave the profession before their fifth year.[4]

You are not a candle or a tool or an endless well of patience and productivity. You are a person with needs and emotions and limitations, and acknowledging them will actually make all of this work more possible, not less.

Ultimately, the only part of this work fully within your control is how you show up to work every day and what you do with yourself while you're there. Most allyship (and survival) within education is practicing your ability to emotionally regulate yourself. When we feel dysregulated at school, meaning we feel emotionally volatile, thin, and unpredictable, it rubs off on our students. They can feel when we are impatient, irritable, frustrated, and frazzled. While many of us can "mask" through these feelings, that masking takes its toll too. Because then not only are we feeling heavy and unmanageable feelings, but we're also doing the additional heavy lifting of pretending we are not. And when we do that over and over and over again, our mask wears down. That's when burnout sets in.

If we want to hold space for all our students, not even just our queer students, we need to start seeing our individual emotional well-being as a critical part of that effort.

Often that means doing less, not more.

It's only through real rest and unconditional compassion for ourselves that we can start making room for that kind of healing.

Now if we can only get that funded as quickly as a new computer lab or homecoming fireworks, we'll be all set.

Notes

1. Moyerbrailean, Anne, "Neurodivergence in the LGBTQ+ Community," Pride Center of VT, December 21, 2021, https://www.pridecentervt.org/2021/12/22/neurodivergence-in-the-lgbtq-community/

2. Czachor, Emily Mae, "Major Brands Scaled Back Pride Month Campaigns in 2024. Here's Why that Matters." CBS News, June 29, 2024, https://www.cbsnews.com/news/pride-month-campaigns-2024-major-brands-scaled-back-why-that-matters/

3. Colvin, Caroline, "Which Companies have Dropped DEI so far?" HR Dive, September 18, 2024, https://www.hrdive.com/news/the-companies-that-have-dropped-dei-programming-recently/727373/

4. Cineas, Fabiola, "Are Teachers Leaving the Classroom En Masse?" Vox, August 18, 2022, https://www.vox.com/policy-and-politics/2022/8/18/23298916/teacher-shortages-debate-local-national

CHAPTER SEVEN

The Mental Environment

The Space Within the Space

I first started to feel like an established teacher when I was no longer parroting what my former and supervising teachers had modeled for me but had my own unique fingerprint in the way I started each day. Additionally, I'm autistic, which means I often lean into a behavior called *echolalia*, or the comforting repetition of sounds or phrases. This means I'm a sucker for a good language routine. One of my favorites was (and still is) the way I asked my students for feedback before they started an activity on their own:

> "Alright everybody, before we get started, does anyone have any questions, comments, concerns, queries, quandaries, complaints, or compliments?"

Not only was it fun to say, but many of my students also liked saying it along with me, and the list got longer from year to year. It also helped a ton with the weird silence so many of us are used to when we ask for questions. Now that silence was filled with students asking things like "What's a quandary?" or "Am I allowed to be concerned about this whole book?" While silly, they usually created a wide enough buffer that a student with a real question was able to raise their hand and ask it before we got started.

All this to say: this is the environment – the mental environment – that has a chance to make another home for your queer students, and it's just as important as the physical one. And whether it's shifting some of your established classroom language or adding some habits that foster a more flexible space, these changes have the potential for some high returns on a small investment. So, let's get started!

On the Way in the Door

On my campus, it was actively encouraged that teachers started our day standing at the door to greet students as they arrived. While it wasn't super popular with teachers who would rather be prepping for their next lesson or taking 30 seconds to catch up on emails, it was a policy that I never had a hard time getting behind. We taught a six-period day, and I did my absolute best to prop my door open and greet my kids this way every period of the day, every day of the week. There are some obvious, and then some less obvious, reasons why.

The first and clearest is that it's an opportunity to establish rapport. I have always had a hard time remembering names, and watching students jog down the hall to my class was a good chance for me to practice as I learned what was going on in the world outside of my room. While it's brief, one-on-one time with students outside of the classroom was the perfect opportunity to hear about what was happening in other classes, which students were friends with other students, who was meeting up over the weekend, who was breaking up, who was running late, and who might need a little bit of extra attention.

Because this is where good teaching for all students meets teaching like an ally: standing in the doorway is an excellent opportunity for intervention. Once class starts, all bets are off – the chaos of the lesson, the standards, the clock, and competition with 40 other young adults means that students who might need to be noticed fade quickly into the background. But if you make it a habit to really take your time in the doorway; to ask how they're doing; to check in about their time in other classes, sports, or the school play; to not rush them through but develop a routine of care – it becomes shorthand for "I give a shit about you."

The doorway became where I learned about absolutely everything, even if I didn't grab the whole story right away.

Because a student who is right on the edge of tears can put a hood up, sink low in their desk, and hide behind a book for 90 minutes. The last thing they want is to be found out in a quiet moment only to lose it in front of all their classmates. For many kids, especially once they make it to high school, the social consequences of breaking down emotionally are high enough not to ask for help.

But if I'm at the door, watching as they approach and greeting them before they walk inside, I have a chance to tell that something is wrong before they're socially spotlighted. I can ask if they would mind waiting just a moment, poke my head in the room to get my students started on bell work, and then talk to them in the relative privacy of the hallway. And I might not be able to help – sometimes it's not any deeper than "my boyfriend saw my text but hasn't responded," which is both beneath and beyond my abilities – but they know now that at least one adult cares enough to ask. Even when we're grown, it's easy for us to write an internal narrative when we're struggling. We can spiral into "no one cares about me" territory very quickly, especially when we don't have the emotional tools to soothe ourselves. The doorway gives us a chance to disrupt the narrative, which is that much more prominent when you're a queer kid and you constantly see the ways in which your needs are sidelined.

And the doorway is a chance for allyship across countless experiences and identities for your students. I taught a neurodivergent sophomore who sometimes had "nonverbal" days, when it was much harder for him to speak. The doorway was where he would hand me a sticky note to let me know it was one of those days. And during the height of teaching during COVID-19, a group of virus-conscious students developed a complex "no hands handshake" that they exchanged with me every morning. Instead of any kind of skin contact, we jumped in unison and tapped our shoes together. It was silly, we looked ridiculous, and it's a daily routine that I miss very much.

Ultimately, while most teachers have at least one strategy to develop rapport and intervention points for their students, it's worth finding one where it's clear that no one is left behind.

Shifting Classroom Language

Changing the language we use in the classroom is deceptively simple. People are creatures of habit, and we lock ourselves into patterns of thinking that are exceptionally challenging to reroute, especially as we get older. There are members of my own family who, though they support me, my life, and my work, still can't forge a lasting connection between their brains and their mouths when they talk about me. Even when my booming Rick Astley voice comes through the telephone to them, they trip over the "shes" and "hers" that they've used for me since I was born. Thirty-plus years of wiring are hard to untangle.

But there's a real benefit to taking this task on in your own classroom. Committing to a few pointed shifts will make the environment more affirming and welcoming for your LGBTQ+ students and do the heavy lifting of modeling cognitive flexibility for everyone else.

Let's start with an easy one:

> Instead of saying, "Good morning, *Ladies and Gentlemen!*"
> or
> "Hello, *Boys and Girls!*"

Skip the binary thinking and sub in one or more of these options:

- Friends
- Scholars
- Learners

Or get more specific with age groups, your content area, or your school's mascot:

8th graders

Sophomores

Scientists

Dancers

Vaulters

Mathematicians

Authors

Scorpions

Vikings

Or, if you're like me, you can get a little more creative:

Friends, Romans, Countrymen

Princes of Maine, Kings of New England

Party People and/or Poopers

If anything, those last options gave us a fun jumping-off point for the day and got students talking in the early hours of the morning! Of course, one of the more uncomfortable changes, especially for language teachers, will be the choice to lean more heavily on the singular gender-neutral pronoun *they*.

Let's get this out of the way first: "they" is a perfectly acceptable singular pronoun, meaning that you are more than welcome to use it to describe just one person and not a group of people. We do it all the time without thinking, and it's likely that you even did it today.

Imagine someone cuts you off on the way to school, barely missing your front bumper, before speeding off through a red light. You're talking to someone on the phone (hands free, of course) and want to describe what just happened. What do you say?

Or you're walking through the park with a picnic lunch and you're looking for an open table. There's only one available, but someone has left a pair of sunglasses on the bench. You hold them up and shout to anyone around to find out whose they might be. What do you say?

It's likely your answers look like this:

> "This person just came out of nowhere and almost hit me! Then **they** just drove away like nothing happened! **They're** going to get **themselves** hurt for sure."

And

> "Did anyone leave **their** sunglasses here? If **they** want them back, I'll leave them on the table!"

The number of people who have looked me – a veteran English Language teacher – in the face and said, "I can't use 'they' because it's not grammatically correct" is as vast as it is infuriating. If you're still torn, consider the following:

- "They" is accepted as a singular gender-neutral pronoun by the Modern Language Association (MLA), the Chicago Manual of Style (CMOS), and the Associated Press (AP), which are essentially the golden trifecta of English linguistic authorities.
- "They" has been used as a singular pronoun in writing since at least the fourteenth century, and authors who have used it include William Shakespeare, Charles Dickens, Geoffrey Chaucer, Emily Dickinson, Jane Austen, and F. Scott Fitzgerald.
- I said it's okay, and I wrote this book.

If you do nothing else after reading this but widen your acceptance for "they" in your heart, I'll call it a win.

This can extend into your classroom in several ways, but I most strongly suggest these top priorities:

- No longer marking a singular "they" as grammatically incorrect on student work.
- Opting for "they" over "his or her/he or she" in your own speaking and writing.
- Practicing and using "they/them" pronouns for students who ask.
- Training your writers to opt for "they" when describing the work or writing of an author, speaker, or artist whose gender you do not know.

This will take some practice and intention, but it's an effort that will pay off, especially for your queer students. For language, teaching like an ally just means moving away from wording that makes assumptions. It's within these assumptions that LGBTQ+ students find themselves consistently pushed into the margins, and language is a powerful tool for both inflicting and reversing that unique kind of pain.

Swerving Around the Power Struggle

Queer students already live in a world rooted squarely in shame. As teachers, we become better allies when we shed shame from as many of our teaching practices as possible. You might think that shame is entirely absent from your classroom, but it has its ways of sneaking in. We turn to it mostly when we feel out of control, because it can be effective in the short term for maintaining order, but it doesn't do much to foster connection or address any of the underlying needs that so many behaviors stem from.

Most systems of reward and punishment come from shame, which I know is hard to hear. Mostly, what we're doing when we present our students with extrinsic motivators that don't have any natural connection to the behavior we're hoping for is training our students to barter praise and acceptance for compliance. Shame creeps in when we remember that a "problem behavior" is usually a result of an unmet need, and if kids get too used to ignoring their needs to please an authority figure, we're setting them up for unhappy (and even potentially abusive) relationships with everyone from bosses to romantic partners down the line.

Marble jars, clip charts, classroom stores – these are all our attempts at bargaining with children because we know we're outnumbered, and we want even just a single moment of peace. Yes, it's true that even as adults we swap work and compliance for rewards (a paycheck, benefits, vacation time) and to avoid punishment (losing our jobs), but we also have the choice to opt in and out of different systems when we find out they work or don't work for us. We have a lot of different places in which we have the chance to find belonging, and we also have fully formed adult brains that have the capacity to divorce our work performance from our inherent sense of self-worth (even if we don't always do it well). Kids don't.

When their needs clash with ours, we can end up in a classic classroom power struggle, especially for those of us who are fortunate enough to teach the grades in which students are first starting to recognize and exercise their autonomy. And while there's no data telling us that queer students end up in disciplinary situations more often than their peers, we do know that marginalized students are much more likely to face suspension or expulsion than their classmates and that disruptive behaviors often stem from unchecked anger, fear, and emotional dysregulation. The argument here is not to just *accept* classroom disruptions and disrespect from your students but to pivot to a new kind of strategy whenever it's necessary to address it.

So, if we set the scene:

> You are teaching your class, maybe lecturing at the front of the room, maybe doing the "teacher wander" with your hands locked behind your back as you observe your students during quiet study time when, suddenly, a wild behavior appears!

In this scenario, the behavior would have to be above just "a little annoying" but below "call for backup." Maybe it's a rude comment to you, a disregard for a critical classroom policy, or even a verbal insult directed at a classmate. In most classrooms, what comes next could easily become a power struggle. With all eyes on the two of you, your student will likely feel backed into a corner if you try to engage head on. These conflicts often turn into a "you versus them" situation, where you are attempting to convince them to submit to your authority or else there will be a consequence. The student has no room for honesty or vulnerability here, because they're faced with a hard decision: bow down and apologize to you, potentially losing them the credibility of their peers, or push back to save face, likely escalating well beyond what either of you want.

And while the teacher usually "wins," either when the consequence gets too high for the student to face or when it's progressed to the point of outside intervention from an administrator or campus supervisor, actually no one wins. "Winning" might mean that the teacher has retained all the power, but the relationship between the two of you is now broken, or at least flexed to its limit. It will be hard to build trust again.

Remember, we're talking about *Teaching Like an Ally* here. Trust is the beginning and end of the game. You have no idea who might need you later or who is looking for a single adult who might understand them. And that's discounting completely the 40 students who just watched you go toe-to-toe with a 15-year-old. Even if that kid is destined to blow you off, their classmates might think twice about trusting you now too.

The alternative I'm about to offer won't work 100 percent of the time, but like everything else in this book, it's about *trying*. It doesn't have to always work to be effective. Again, what are you modeling for the average 60–80 eyeballs following your every move?

Instead of giving in to the power struggle, *take it outside*.

And do it right away.

The moment your teenage adversary starts to tilt into whatever behavior is disrupting class, ask them if they wouldn't mind stepping outside for just a moment.

The risks here are not zero. Have I had a student "step outside" only to take off for the vending machine? Oh yeah, for sure. But they always come back, and now you have two behaviors to discuss.

The important element here is the diffusion of the tension. This is also why I didn't sub in "stay behind to see me after class" in place of the immediate removal – I need that bad air to clear.

Ask them to step into the hallway (or the outdoors or the learning annex – whatever is beyond your door), but don't follow behind right away. Give them a chance to cool off and regulate themselves before you go after them. It will help them get their head screwed on correctly, and it will give you a moment to get your students set up before you step out. If I didn't have anything right away that would work to occupy them, I usually had them pause for a "quiet journal reflection" on a question I made up on the spot.

Your approach is important. You are the adult, but your authority does not mean you own the air and hold the advantage in every environment. Choose to approach them like you are crossing into *their space*. And here's what you're going to say:

"Hey, so what's going on?"

No judgment, no demand for an apology or a reckoning, just real concern and curiosity.

And you do have to feel it. Faking it doesn't count. Even when it sucks and you're mad, find a way to access a genuine want to learn more about your student. This won't magically transform this moment together into the end of an episode of *7th Heaven*, but it has a high chance of disarming them. Follow up with questions to let them know that you are less concerned about the behavior and more concerned about *them*.

It was challenging to remember that these discussions weren't about me or my feelings. Whenever I was talking through a classroom incident in the hallway, I had to very consciously avoid the phrase "You made me feel _____." Because frankly, this 15-year-old didn't *make me* feel anything.

The point is not to hold a child accountable for your feelings. While this is sometimes an important avenue to explore for empathy and growth, that's not usually how we use it. For the most part, it's a way for us to engage our anger in a way that guilts a kid and absolves us of our responsibility to investigate further.

So instead, really ask "what's going on?" like you want to know, and listen all the way through their answer, without interrupting. Sometimes the answer will be obvious BS, but sometimes it won't. And sometimes, more often than you'd think, the student with the BS answer will come back with a real one later.

And then again, sometimes not.

We aren't looking to bat a thousand here. We're looking to show that there is an adult in their life who cares enough to ask.

When you've wrapped up all you can accomplish and set some ground rules for reentry, let them know that they are welcome to rejoin the class when they're ready.

I would always come back in first so that all the most curious eyes would fall on me first. If I timed it right, I could move the class on to the next activity as my student returned, saving them the hassle of being watched.

Will this exact scenario work as mapped for your very specific situation? Nope, probably not. But this is, ideally, a good starting point as you evaluate what you want moments like this to look like for you moving forward.

Let's Take a Walk

Almost every transformational one-on-one I ever had with a student after a "problem" behavior was on a walk, and I only ever took walks when something was feeling *very* off about them.

This was usually when a student whose typical behavior would shift dramatically from engaged, excited, studious, or kind to something radically different. This usually looked like a major incident of plagiarism or a volatile change in the way they acted toward me or another one of their classmates. And while sometimes these walks happened during a passing period or lunch, they often interfered directly with the instructional day. That's why flexibility was built into my pedagogy. Ultimately, nothing was ever more important than the safety and emotional well-being of my students. The curriculum could always survive a 15-minute change in plans.

And no, I am not advocating for abandoning your students within an unsupervised classroom. This is only a viable strategy with a support team. For me, I had an understanding with a handful of teachers in my building. When one of us needed a moment of coverage, for a bathroom break, an IEP meeting, or a quick hallway dissociation, it was a no-questions-asked deal from whomever was on a break. If that's not viable for you, consider talking with your admin team about coverage from either them or another campus supervisor. If not, lunch it is.

Walks with students provide a kind of "public privacy" that protects the both of you. You can remain visible, and with the immediate ability to call for backup, while giving them the space to talk without the fear of being overheard.

It's on walks like these that I found out where some of these concerning behaviors were coming from:

- The Mormon student who realized he was gay and reckoning with the fact that he was likely about to lose the support of his entire family.
- The AP student who, that weekend, had caught her mother cheating with another man and whose mother was now bribing her for her silence.
- The freshman whose parent had left on a business trip two weeks ago and, as they'd learned moments before my class, was choosing never to return.

All these moments would have been a mystery to me, and likely every other adult in their life, if I hadn't found a way to ask.

We train kids very early to ignore their needs and to hide how they are feeling while they are at school. From scheduled bathroom breaks and strict boundaries about eating to mandates against speaking for long periods of time, they learn that their feelings and their bodies are not trustworthy and that they won't be listened to or regarded if they advocate for themselves. While it can be tempting to ask "Why would you do this?" and "What is your problem?," it's maybe more helpful to wonder, "What is the need here? What are we ignoring?"

Because it's in our ability to see and address our students' less obvious needs that the material fluff of a typical "safe space" becomes superfluous. While I love introducing the young people in my life to queer books and I savor every time a teenager smiles at my rainbow laptop sticker, the real lasting gift for LGBTQ+ youth is a chance at self-acceptance, self-compassion, and self-love. None of those personal milestones is possible when a child is steeped in shame.

PART III

Inside the Classroom

CHAPTER EIGHT

Classroom Policies

WTF Is a Safe Space?

We talk a lot about "emotional safety" in education but rarely take the time to break down exactly what that is supposed to mean. If you ask a particular flavor of embittered veteran teachers what a "safe space" is, they'll tell you it's the conclusion of a lifetime of coddling; a protective shelter that keeps our youth from facing the harsh and inevitable realities of the "real world." And sometimes they're right. When executed poorly, we can stumble into hosting exclusive and limited environments that act as echo chambers, removing us from the real lived experiences of the communities we're attempting to serve. I've hosted Queer Student Alliance meetings in my classroom for more than a decade, and I have seen conversations between young people devolve into what we sometimes call the "Oppression Olympics," where students trade traumas for the purpose of earning the chance to be the last and singular person left with the authority to complain. These dialogues lean heavily on semantics, skipping over the chance for listening and connection completely in favor of arguments about identities, labels, and who has permission to call themselves what. It gets tiring quickly.

What you might notice about that version of a "safe space" is that nobody gets to feel particularly safe. Because really, it doesn't matter how many flags are on the door or how many signs declare that a room is an "open and welcoming environment for all," the responsibility for engineering and maintaining that space lies squarely with us. Emotional safety is much more complex than the reductionist view that assumes we simply roll students up in bubble wrap to protect their feelings and shield them from criticism. If we want our schools and classrooms to operate with everyone within them feeling individually secure and empowered, we have to land somewhere in the middle: with enough structure and clarity to define what we expect and accept from our students, but with the right amount of flexibility to give them room to grow on their own.

So, wtf is a safe space, and how do you maintain one? Here are some solid starting parameters:

A Safe Space Rejects the Paradox of Tolerance

The paradox of tolerance is a tricky pitfall that dooms us before we begin if we let it slip between the cracks. Essentially, the argument is that if we tolerate intolerance, intolerance eventually takes over, exterminating the tolerant and the practice of tolerance with them. More simply, if we create a "safe space" for both sheep and wolves, we only have a safe space for wolves. Bigotry has a way of dressing up the tools of progressive ideology and using them in bad faith, and it works well if we aren't prepared to spot it and shut it down, which is much easier in some circumstances than it is in others.

I think a lot about the place of "free speech" within the paradox of tolerance and how groups like student newspapers, who are just beginning to understand the place of journalistic responsibility, get tricked into platforming bad actors when they think they're operating in the name of balance and fairness. "We have to hear from both sides" works a lot better, say, when you're planning a center spread about homecoming themes and the pros and cons of expanding the student parking lot than when fielding article submissions about the basic rights and personhood of trans people. "Free speech" is a guarantee against being jailed for your opinions, not a promise of a soap box to stand on or a captive audience to lecture to. It is completely fair to hold boundaries against hate in student spaces, and strong outlines that detail what specifically falls outside of those boundaries are helpful in setting and maintaining expectations early.

A Safe Space Differentiates Between Discomfort and Danger

Even if we really wish we could, we just can't promise our students that they will never experience discomfort or pain when they are at school, and being up front with them about it with clarity and compassion goes a long way. For many of your students, especially the ones who hold one or more marginalized identities, the expectation of complete safety would be borderline delusional, and they know it. Instead of promising something you can't completely control, be direct about what it is you do have influence over and clue them in as often as it is possible to do so. Let them know that while you aren't able to step between them and every challenging situation, you will show up even when it puts you out or causes you discomfort.

For many of us, what often makes us feel the most secure is information. I had a student one year who had survived an incident of mass violence, and she disclosed to me early in the year that campus-wide drills often caused her an incredible amount of pain. Though she wasn't in any real danger during those drills, her pain was real. I couldn't save her from the anxiety of the drill, but what I could do was go out of my way to tell her in the morning when I knew one was coming. I also worked it out with her other teachers, so she was allowed to gather with my class on the football field when we did any mock evacuations. When she was with me, I could tell her what I knew when I knew it, and it soothed some of the worst parts of her fear.

A Safe Space Manages Time Reliably

It might feel a little out of left field to see "thoughtful time management" on a list of what makes a classroom emotionally safe, but it's one of the most critical and oft overlooked pieces to this puzzle, especially for rooms that feature any kind of whole-class or group discussion. Too often do we put hours into designing the perfect lesson only for it to wither in practice because we forgot to check the clock. For newer teachers, managing class time can feel like an impossible battle, but it really does get easier the longer you do it. Knowing exactly how much time has passed without glancing at a watch is still one of my favorite superpowers.

So why is budgeting time effectively part of developing emotional safety in the classroom? First, consider how time is used in your room. How much of your 50 or 100 minutes is allocated to students listening to you? How much is set aside for them to listen to each other, or for you to listen to them? For students to feel secure and heard, they need to have the time to share and speak. There's just no way to learn anything about your students if you don't have room to hear them. For class discussions, there needs to be enough time built into the lesson for students to speak more than once and for quieter students to develop the courage to add to the discourse started by their peers. Remember, children who have the most anxiety around chiming in during a discussion will almost always save their additions for the end of class. Nothing is more demoralizing for students like that than being cut off by the bell. Be generous with time when you can, and try to build consistent protocols around communicating that timing to your class.

A Safe Space Models and Respects Boundaries

Boundaries has become a bit of a buzzword in mental health spaces over the last couple of years, and it's a little muddled as to what it means to have and enforce your own boundaries. A *boundary* is not controlling what people say or how they act but instead how you react and respond. A teacher with no boundaries is a recipe for burnout, and it usually means that you haven't really taken the time to reflect and be honest about what chars your biscuit.

When I was leading long class discussions every week in my language and composition classes, I encouraged students to request topics that were meaningful and relevant to their lives, but I was also up front about my own boundaries as their facilitator. I told them that because I had a family history with homelessness, even offhand comments that came off as callous to people experiencing homelessness were likely to get me heated. Instead of making my students responsible for those feelings (I would never say they "made" me feel anything), I let them know that I might have to step back or take a moment to myself if I started to feel my feathers getting ruffled. Because realistically, teenagers are going to push boundaries, and it should feel safe to test their opinions with their peers. They aren't in charge of holding my feelings for me, but I am also a person who will feel things regardless. By being clear and modeling what a boundary might look like, they had a guide for how to create and communicate boundaries for themselves.

A Safe Space Shares Responsibility for Norms

This one probably won't come as a surprise, as collectively creating classroom guidelines has taken off in education circles as a great start-of-year activity, from pre-K through secondary. Students are much more likely to feel a shared responsibility for a classroom's culture if they had a hand in drafting how that should look, and it's pretty simple to set this up and scaffold for any group of students at any age. I would start (on a whiteboard or with some chart paper) by discussing and agreeing on what behavior is necessary for a class to operate successfully. What does a good learning environment look like? What makes learning harder? I always liked asking this in small groups and then writing their contributions on the board and seeing where we all agree. From there, students can share what class policies and guidelines will be the most effective for creating the environment everyone wants. Have students help create a cute poster that stays up throughout the year and *voilà*.

I would say that being told what to do is abhorrent to most kids, but really, it's not something many adults appreciate either. It's hard to feel emotionally safe in an environment where you have zero agency. And any time you can offer students choices or control over their own space, it adds considerably to their personal sense of security.

A Safe Space Enforces Consequences

If your school has a policy against cyberbullying, but it becomes clear that they don't enforce it, then you do not have a policy against cyberbullying. Students learn very quickly if rules have teeth, and they adjust accordingly. Much like a toddler who learns that nothing happens after their mom counts down from 3, policies that aren't backed up with consistent and enforceable consequences become useless for the students they are meant to protect. Equally, a policy with a consequence that is skirted or avoided because teachers or administrators don't want to handle the fallout or paperwork that comes with enforcing it might as well be struck from the student handbook completely.

This is why it is critical that every adult on a given campus is on the same page with policies and their consequences. For a long time, our school had a ruthless attendance and tardy policy. The guideline was that if a student was not across the threshold of their class by the time the bell rang, they were sent up to the attendance office for a lunch detention slip. It didn't matter whose fault it was or what great excuse they had – if they were late, they spent 20 minutes of their lunch in a classroom supervised by a staff volunteer. Though it wasn't a perfect system, it was effective. After a while, the edges began to fray. Teachers began to get emails to excuse tardies across the board for the first 5–10 minutes of class. Whispers spread that some teachers would grant their students an extra couple of minutes after lunch. Soon, arguments started in classrooms where the policy was still being followed to the letter. Teachers got tired of the fights, and many stopped enforcing the rule altogether.

Now scale that example for the policies meant to protect the emotional safety of students. If your campus advertises that they are a "hate-free" environment, what policies back that up? What are the consequences, and who enforces them? And what are the effects for your most threatened student populations when that system breaks down?

For Safety or Control?

Now is a good time to look at the policies and systems that compose your classroom. For each of them, ask yourself: "Is this a policy that provides me and my students with emotional or physical safety, or is it just a policy that provides me with control?"

It can be hard to spot the difference, but the distinction is an important one. Classrooms are chaotic places, and it can be all we can do sometimes to keep our rooms from devolving into the later chapters of *The Lord of the Flies*, but when we prioritize our need for calm, quiet, and order without considering how that might be affecting the social and emotional development of our students, we're primed to miss the opportunity for a more subtle version of allyship.

For example, I used to have a strict late-work policy.

At my most rigid, I was teaching classrooms of advanced English students that maxed at almost 40 kids in a period, and I had foolishly agreed to a 6/5ths schedule. For the uninitiated, this means that in each school day, I was teaching about 240 students from 7 a.m. to 3 p.m. with zero breaks. The late-work policy, which slashed work to 50% credit if it was turned in even seconds after the deadline, was mostly there to help me keep a desperate hold on my own sanity. I just didn't have capacity for a dozen conversations a day asking for exceptions and special consideration. I shut them all down. I rationalized this policy to myself as preparing my students for the "real world" (there's that "real world" again, as if my kids lived in the Matrix now), but part of me knew that wasn't true. Grace exists in the real world. People are granted extensions and second chances all the time, and rarely are we faced with stern and inflexible people who are unwilling to work with us when we need compassion. Even if that weren't the case, the last thing I would want to do is convince hundreds of young people a year that it's expected and advisable to *be* those stern and inflexible people.

The next year, I dropped the extra class, and I changed my policy.

For many teachers, it can be important to us to be perceived as serious. We want our colleagues and our students to see our courses as competitive and challenging. We like to think that if our class is hard and we are tough, that's a good indication of how much our students will learn and how valuable our lessons are.

But that's not true.

What's more likely is that our most intense policies are shutting out the students who need us the most. There are kids who can't keep up with late work, who struggle under the weight of unmanageable workloads, who aren't showing up to school on time, and who aren't able to attend optional study sessions and complete hours of homework a night. Many of these students are disabled, are living below the poverty line, are unhoused, or are foster youth, queer, neurodivergent, and/or BIPOC.[i] The students who rise above those barriers aren't necessarily smarter, more committed, or more capable; they are usually just better resourced.

And this was my experience. I was the student who would have been most hurt by the same policies I was enforcing in my classroom. As a high school kid, I spent a handful of years living with a mother who moved around a lot. I wasn't doing homework after school because I was tagging along with her on city buses or letting myself into an empty house and finding a way to put my own dinner together. I didn't need harsher policies; I needed a teacher who had the time to see that I needed empathy and support.

---

[i] Black, indigenous, and people of color.

That's not to say that every policy is a bad policy – it's just worth glancing through your syllabus and having an honest conversation about who is most benefited by the policies you do have, and why.

Setting Expectations and Evaluating Policies

While there are some common classroom policies that disproportionately affect your queer students, generally the guidelines that benefit them also benefit everyone else. The inverse is also true: policies harmful to queer students are probably not doing any favors for their straight and cisgender peers. Though we're often accused of accessing "special treatment," there are no reasonable updates or adjustments here that will do anything other than level up your classroom game for anyone lucky enough to take your class. The rising tide lifts all boats.

Here's a breakdown of some common classroom policies and procedures that might need an update, and some suggestions for how to start.

Attendance Procedures

I have only worked within school climates that take attendance very seriously. Because California ties school site funding to daily student numbers, the most ruthless and tenacious people on campus always worked at the attendance window. Forget to submit your absences in the first 10 minutes of class? Get ready for at least three emails and a phone call before you've had a chance to explain the first activity of the day. For this reason, I developed airtight attendance procedures early in my career and refined them to an exact science over more than a decade.

An allied attendance process starts at the beginning of the year, the very first time you meet your new crop of students. This is especially true when you teach secondary school and have to contend with five or six groups of 30+ children and the first day of school is a panicked whirlwind of new names in an already packed and chaotic schedule. This usually means we are more likely to lean on systems that have worked for us in the past without evaluating if they're still what's best for us or our kids. Classically, students file in, choose a seat, and the teacher stands in front of the room to read each name in alphabetical order. Students respond with "here," the teacher marks them as present, and the school day continues. It's simple, efficient, and the most anxiety-inducing strategy that you could possibly pick for a queer (more acutely and specifically a transgender) student.

It is likely that a trans student is still listed by their deadname[ii] on your school's attendance roster. Even if they come from a supportive and proactive family, updating a legal name takes time and money (in the state of California, updating a first name costs $400 and bounces around the court system for 4–6 months before becoming official), and school administrative systems are notoriously slow. When I changed my name, it was two years before the change was reflected on student class locator cards.

For this reason, waiting to hear your teacher out[iii] you, potentially up to six or seven times, is highly stressful. While more social and proactive students may reach out to a teacher ahead of time to ask them explicitly to use another name, it is rare to find a child (or adult) who is willing to face that kind of potential confrontation, especially on the first day of school. Even queer students who do not identify as trans might still feel this heightened anxiety. There are many young people who are exploring their own relationship to gender or might present or look atypical when compared to the "M" or "F" often listed beside their name on the attendance sheet. They might use a nickname or prefer to

---

[ii] Refers to the name a transgender person was given at birth but no longer uses in their own life. It can also be used as a verb, as in "deadnaming," or the action of using a trans person's former name. It is generally considered to be not only rude, but often dangerous, to ask for or use a trans person's deadname.

[iii] To "out" someone means to expose them as LGBTQ+ without their consent. Even if a student is "out" to their friends and family, they still might not want relative strangers to know their gender identity or sexual orientation, and ultimately, they get to decide if, when, and how people learn about them.

go by a name that less sharply questions their presentation. A sportier or more masculine "Alexandra" may prefer "Alex" and feel a version of dysphoria[iv] with her birth name even if she doesn't consider herself trans.

Realistically, there are hundreds of reasons why the traditional "Call and response" attendance procedure sets the wrong tone for the kind of environment you're hoping to curate in your classroom. I tried several iterations of this over the years and managed to narrow down to a system that worked well.

Instead of standing in front of the classroom with a clipboard, prop your door open and greet students as they appear. I almost always ended up with a line into the hallway when I did this, but I started as early as possible to keep it as short as I could. For each student you meet, tell them your name and the class you teach (this will also help cut down on students who wander into your room by accident), and then ask for their last name. Use your pen to mark them as "present" when you find them on your list, and as you're looking, *ask what name they would like you to use for them this year*.

I like this phrase for several reasons:

- It doesn't assume that only transgender students have a preferred name.

- It signals right from the jump that you recognize, and will respect, their autonomy.

- It allows you to practice pronouncing their name with them before you use it in front of their classmates.

- It makes space for students you may have had in the past to come to you with a new name this year.

[iv] Though dysphoria can mean a general sense of unease or dissatisfaction, it is often used within "gender dysphoria" to describe the feeling of discomfort and mismatch between a gender assigned at birth and a current lived experience with gender.

Will this potentially eat into the first couple of minutes of class time? Yeah, but you were going to use that time for attendance anyway. Handling it at the doorway means you can keep an eye on the students milling about your classroom while still giving them the chance to get comfortable without you, and you will likely even save time by minimizing transitions for both you and them.

It's a win-win, win, win.

Throughout the year, attendance becomes less (but not entirely) important. I kept a seating chart pinned to the clipboard that I kept on my front podium and used that as my reference when I needed it. Though I sometimes wrote little notes to myself about students (number of absences, marks to remind me to email parents, etc.), I never wrote down anything that would damage a student if it were to fall into the wrong hands. If I suspected (or knew for sure) that a student was queer or trans, that was never committed to paper. Unless told explicitly otherwise by the student themselves, I knew not to assume that anything was public knowledge.

Bathroom Policies

Over the course of my career, I have taught, mentored, and coached *A LOT* of transgender students. Many people are surprised by the most common afflictions they face at school, and I haven't seen any studies that have taken the time to examine them. The problems might seem unrelated until you glance back at the heading for this section, and they are *dehydration and bladder infections*.

The truth is that many trans students would rather cause serious harm to their own bodies than use the bathroom at school. In fact, most students who face harassment at school will do everything in their power to avoid the bathroom. Consider:

- There is no consistent adult supervision in the bathroom.
- Peers who are looking for a place to do anything ill-advised or illegal will often set up headquarters in a student bathroom.

- There are a strict set of unspoken social rules to navigate in a bathroom.
- There are no cameras and often very few witnesses.

For a trans student, that's a dangerous enough situation on its own. Throw in the now decades-long battle centered entirely over their right to pee where they are most comfortable and secure, and you have a prefabricated anxiety that follows them any time they exist in a public space. I think so often now about Nex Benedict, the 16-year-old nonbinary Oklahoma student who lost their life in 2024 after a bathroom altercation gone south. It is, quite simply, one of the most dangerous places on your campus for a trans or gender nonconforming student.

As a teacher, I also know how frustrating it can be to manage the endless carousel of students who want to interrupt class time to "use the bathroom." Every moment out of class means that a child may be missing a critical bit of information or skill practice, and I can still feel that familiar stomach pit drop when a raised hand was not a thoughtful and innovative contribution to a lesson like I hoped but instead a bored "cannigotothuhbathroom?" from someone who hadn't been paying attention to begin with.

I also know how we can reason ourselves in knots about how it's not our responsibility to manufacture space for restroom breaks. Students have a break, a lunch, and usually about 10 minutes to move from one class to the next, which is plenty of time for anyone with a typical bladder to make it to a toilet before they're expected at their next class.

But it's not quite that simple.

For many students, using the bathroom between classes is a no-go. If it's typically stressful to brave a restroom when you know it might out you to anyone who sees you, the absolute worst time to try is when it will be the most crowded, which is also when every single one of your teachers expects you to go. For a crowded campus, potential lines of their peers add to that stress, and it is much more likely that a student outside of typical gender expectations would rather face the consequences of an annoyed teacher, or even of an inevitable bladder infection.

This is why, as much as it disrupts the flow of class, it is advised to have a flexible and accessible bathroom policy. The following are other considerations:

- **Maintaining at least two bathroom passes, not one:** Though it makes sense on paper to release a single student at a time to the restroom, it can turn any students waiting for their turn into unwitting hostages, especially when the child who's just left the room with the sole pass has a high likelihood of getting "lost" on the way there or back.

- **Degendering your bathroom passes:** Some teachers try to maintain a semblance of order with multiple passes by designating one of them the "girl" pass and the other the "boy" pass. I'm hoping you're far enough into this book by now to see why that might be ill advised.

- **Nixing extra credit points for bathroom passes:** It is not an Olympic achievement to hold your pee, and it's not a great standard to set to ask our students to ignore the body's basic functioning for the chance at a reward.

Bathroom policy overhauls can be a pain point for some teachers because it's one of the only areas where we have a stricter set of guidelines for ourselves than we have for our students. We might think, "We can't just slip out of our rooms whenever we want to empty our bladders, so why should they?"

In this case, it's worth pondering whether restricting their freedom and autonomy might have more to do with satisfying our own resentment than anything else.

Student Check-Ins and Surveys

During the height of COVID lockdowns and distance learning (a phrase that still kicks my nervous system into fight or flight), I learned to find a deep and abundant love in my heart for check-ins.

In my classes, a check-in was a quick online form I slapped together that I intended to use as a shoddy replacement for the kind of one-on-one attention I was used to giving my students. Within it I asked simple questions like "What are you looking forward to this week?" or "What class are you struggling with the most right now?" along with sillier queries such as "If you could be any kind of ecosystem, which would you be, and why?"

The most essential version of a check-in is the classic "beginning of the school year student survey,"[v] which can help immeasurably in your never-ending quest to knowing who your students are as individual people.

This survey is also a great time to learn more about your students' unique circumstances. I used to use this as my venue to learn my students' pronouns, but as national sensitivities shifted, I changed up how I asked. While originally the question was a "required" field and looked like this:

"What are your pronouns?

He/him, she/her, they/them, something else (fill in)"

That didn't last long. Early in the school year, I didn't have enough of an established trust for the question to mean much. Many students felt pressured to answer when they didn't know how I would respond, and more pernicious children would fill in their pronouns with some variation of "I am an Apache attack helicopter."

Eventually, I made the question optional, with a disclaimer that explained why I was asking and how I would use the information they gave to me.

In areas with guidelines that prohibit teachers from asking this question (typing that out made my soul evacuate my body, and it is now floating 3 feet above my laptop), there's a simple workaround for any educators who still want the opportunity to learn about and respect how their students would like to be addressed. Instead of asking directly, add some version of the following instructions:

"Write a sentence about your typical morning in the third person."

---

[v] Would love a footnote or QR code that takes readers to the downloadable sample version I have linked under "Additional Resources" in the TOC.

If necessary, you can always add the definition of third person and an example of what it looks like to use it. This selection is an opportunity not only to learn your students' pronouns but also. . .

- Avoids the use of the word *pronoun*, which can be triggering for some people and sometimes against a school or state policy
- Allows you to get a solid picture of how your students see and talk about themselves
- Can help you evaluate their basic grasp of writing

In addition to a survey at the start of the year, it can be additionally helpful to return to a similar or even identical version at midyear checkpoints, such as the beginning of a new quarter or semester. Like adults, our students are constantly in flux. They grow and change constantly, and it's always useful to know when those changes are on the horizon.

Notes from the Queer Teacher Survival Guide

Choosing Your Name in the Classroom

Straight and cisgender teachers rarely have to think about what name they want students to use for them throughout their career. Take a last name; stick "Mr," "Ms," or "Mrs" in front of it; and you're golden.

But we have a generally more complicated relationship with names.

For teachers in same-sex partnerships, a changed name means opening a conversation with students about your partner whether you want to or not, and for trans teachers, the decision about when, if ever, to change your name at school is coupled with an unthinkable amount of anxiety.

(Continued)

Before deciding about what to do in regard to your own name, just remember that you do not owe anyone visibility. There is no degree of your life that you have to share with a single other person to live authentically. You are not lying, and you are not being deceitful. Even if you teach in an "accepting" area, this is still a decision that belongs only to you – full stop.

So, what are some options, if you do want a change?

First Name Only: Simple, easy, and removed from the burden of gender. The only cons are that some teachers more advanced in years might think it's too casual for the classroom.

Mx + Last Name: The honorific "Mx" as a replacement for "Mr" or "Ms" has gotten more popular with nonbinary teachers over the last few years. It looks very cool, but you will probably have to repeat yourself a lot at first as colleagues and students practice.

Last Name Only: This was the route I took, and I really enjoyed the simplicity – it saved me a lot of conversations I didn't want to have, and it gave me the handle I've been using online since I started my transition. When anyone asked, "Your name is Flint? Flint what?" I answered, "Just Flint is fine."

Coach/Teacher/Professor/Chef: If you're open to embracing some fun and creativity, there are a whole host of words you can put in front of your name. If you're really feeling fancy, pop back to school for a while and swap to "Dr" permanently.

CHAPTER NINE

The Physical Environment

Check the Space

Remember when we were "taking inventory"? When I asked you to think about what a run-through of the school day might look like from the perspective of one of your queer students? I want to get back into that headspace again for a while.

When you walk into your own classroom, what signs or signals might an LGBTQ+ student see that would tell them that they're in a safe and supportive environment? You might think they aren't looking, especially on the first or second day of school, but they absolutely are. Queer people develop a secondary instinct to scan new spaces for these signs, even when we don't realize it. I'm only conscious that I've done it myself when I feel my shoulders relax and my lungs empty, usually when I spot a rainbow sticker in a shop window, or an "all gender" sign on a public bathroom in a new city. They don't have to be huge gestures to be effective. Generally, we're looking for a hint that we're going to be respected and considered, because there can be huge consequences when we aren't.

Only a few weeks ago, after an unexpected battle with an infection and an unthinkably painful 12-hour wait in an emergency room, I remember looking up at my ER nurse from the fetal position in a terrified haze. I, like many trans people, have grown to really hate medical facilities. At best, we have to navigate a series of very uncomfortable conversations with people who haven't been well trained in our care. At worst, a mishandling of our diagnosis or treatment could kill us, and it does. I looked up at her face first and then down at her name tag, which was decorated with a handful of rainbow stickers and a "she/they" pronoun button.

"Oh, thank god. You're gay," I said, before the pain meds knocked me out.

The stakes aren't quite as high in your classroom, but that doesn't mean they aren't there. In 2019, when I was finishing my master's degree, I decided to focus my research exclusively on the shifts classroom teachers could make to better see and accommodate LGBTQ+ students, especially when it came to their class environment. When I started an extended study of these shifts on my own campus, I began by asking our teachers and about 200 of our students what they thought about the LGBTQ+ student experience at our school (Figure 9.1). Did they agree that queer teenagers likely had it harder, at least during the school day, than their straight and cisgender peers?

The results were telling. Of the 69 surveyed teachers, all except two optioned for "somewhat agree," "agree," or "strongly agree." Their students, however, didn't see it that way: 43% of students answered with either "disagree" or "strongly disagree." There was a disconnect between what the adults and the kids were seeing and experiencing. At least, that's how it seemed.

On the student surveys, however, I left an option for write-in comments. Mixed in with a handful of dismissive (and sometimes downright hateful) thoughts, there were glimmers of kids who were desperate to be seen:

> "I'm really afraid. I can't come out to people without backlash."

> "It can be hard sometimes, especially during debates on LGBTQ stuff, and I just think 'Wow, they hate me for no reason.'"

> "My friend had her car keyed because she's got a lesbian flag in her car. Kids suck."

LGBT (Lesbian, Gay, Bisexual, Transgender) students face a harder time during the school day, either academically or socially.

69 responses

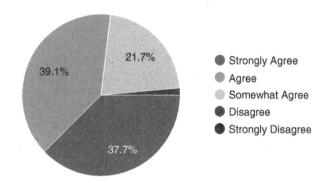

	Strongly Agree	Agree	Somewhat Agree	Disagree	Strongly Disagree
Freshmen (9th)	6.25%	12.50%	31.25%	37.50%	12.50%
Sophomores (10th)	21.88%	25.00%	21.88%	31.25%	0.00%
Juniors (11th)	3.92%	31.37%	35.29%	25.49%	22.58%
Seniors (12th)	13.04%	13.04%	26.09%	34.78%	13.04%
All Students	9.84%	19.69%	29.53%	32.64%	10.88%

FIGURE 9.1 LGBTQ+ student experience survey

So, if we want to start moving the needle for these students, to both make them feel more overtly seen and supported in our classroom, where do we start?

Flags and Signage

> "Isn't putting up a rainbow flag in my classroom showing a preference? I treat all my students the same."

This is, by far, the most pervasive question I get when discussing classroom Pride signage. I heard it a lot when I was still teaching, because one of the most consistent elements of my schoolwide advocacy was making little plastic desktop rainbow flags available to the staff. I would send an email out the week before school – if anyone wanted a flag, I'd be happy to stick a few in their mailbox. Every time, year after year, I would get at least one email with a different version of that question.

So, is a Pride flag "showing a preference?"

Well, no.

If our goal is equity, which is how I read "I treat all of my students the same," that means we want all our students to have equal access to our established markers for student success. As we addressed in some detail in the first section of this book, that's not happening for queer students right now. They are less likely to feel safe and supported at school, less likely to attend, less likely to graduate, less likely to continue to higher education, more likely to experience backlash and bullying, more likely to turn to self-harm and substances, and more likely – by an ever-growing margin – to attempt to end their own lives.

These students are not, practically by any measure, being "treated the same."

For any other group of students experiencing an educational disparity that wide, we build accommodations. Neurodivergent students are allowed extra time on exams or to turn in work, blind students are offered audio or braille materials, and we build ramps for students in wheelchairs. None of these attempts at accessibility is called "showing a preference," because we know they are vital to the success of these students. So why, if we know that LGBTQ+ flags and posters are helpful for our queer students, do we keep having this conversation?

My theory is that this question is a mask for fear.

As teachers, we don't want to admit when we're afraid or when we know deep in our hearts that we are letting that fear push us to act outside of our values. Of the 69 teachers on my campus who answered the staff survey I used for my master's, 76.8% responded that they "strongly agreed" that they were respectful and inclusive of LGBTQ+ students in their classroom, with the rest answering "agree," but only 33.3% answered "strongly agree" when asked if they would be comfortable implementing specific classroom strategies for the benefit of that population.

So, who are we afraid of? The most obvious answer would be parents and families because they sometimes show up to school board meetings to yell about "liberal teacher agendas" and found groups like Moms for Liberty. And I know this might be controversial, but many teachers are also afraid of their students. Sometimes it's a more classic "bullying" fear – we aren't immune from being worn down by the same passive harassment that many of our students face, especially if we're queer ourselves. But, more commonly, many hesitant teachers are afraid of losing relatability and social credibility with their students. Educators are people, and people want to be liked. If there's an atmosphere on campus that being queer isn't cool, there are absolutely teachers who won't be able to access the courage to push back against that narrative.

"So, should I have some kind of flag in my classroom? What are some good options?"

If you can, you should, and I'll tell you why.

As a part of the research I did for my master's, I worked with three different teachers on my campus, all of whom were from different departments, and asked them to try a few different classroom strategies to see how they affected the perspectives of their students. One of the first (and easiest) that everyone agreed to try was putting up Pride flags.

After just a few days, I received an email from a teacher who had chosen to pin a selection of different flags up in her room:

> "Thank you. So, I put the flags on my board, and then I put the big one in my window. My students got so excited and started helping me put them up. . .and then started telling me with pride what flag they were. In my class that came afterward, a bunch of students ran up and started excitedly taking pictures in front, one even exclaiming "I'm so excited I could cry." Amazing what a little bit of a presence can do for kids. I easily had about 20 students come out to me in some form over the course of about 45 minutes. Thought you would want to know."

A day later, I had another email from a different teacher:

> "I've been meaning to write to you.... I have noticed a change in my classroom ever since adding the flags to my walls. I assumed my class was a safe space, but since having those, I have had conversations with students that have made it clear that it wasn't as clearly safe as I had thought. THANK YOU! I am definitely a work in progress."[i]

A rainbow flag isn't a magic wand, but we have some strong evidence that it's a good start. And while there are other options, they might not be quite as effective if they don't come paired with any meaningful context or conversation. For a long time, I was a big advocate for these large glossy posters that were made available to us by a local LGBT Center. They had the words SAFE ZONE in capital letters, and they even made them in a handful of languages. While they were better than nothing, I didn't understand why they weren't hitting quite the same for students. After all, both teachers who sent me those emails already had the signs. Why were their students so excited about the flags?

Why weren't the signs working?

---

[i] Both emails have been edited for anonymity.

The answer, we found in another set of student surveys later, was close to unanimous:

> "They [the flags] feel like something teachers want to do more than something they have to do."

Oh.

The signs, though well-intentioned, were getting lost in all the district-mandated drivel that every teacher was compelled to stick somewhere in their room. The messaging was drowned out by a hundred other flyers, posters for text-a-tip lines, anti-bullying policies, academic integrity statements, and a dozen more platitudes about our school's missions and values.

Sure, the students were saying. *You say you're a safe space for us, but we don't know that you really mean it.*

That doesn't mean that every alternative is a waste of time, just that our intentions have to be loud and clear.

A friend of mine in Colorado teaches on a campus that is set up more like a university than a high school, which means that he and his students don't have a "home base" the way I always did. Instead, he pushes his laptop and a set of textbooks around between rooms on a cart. And while he's not afraid of being conspicuous in his allyship, a 4-foot waving rainbow flag trailing behind him might be a little much. Instead, he has an "ally" sticker on his computer, so it goes where he goes.

Another friend, this time teaching out of a state with strict guidelines prohibiting Pride flags in public schools, had to get a little more creative to help her LGBTQ+ students feel seen and supported. As we were chatting back and forth recently, she had an epiphany about a choice she made months ago:

> "Okay, so I was not allowed to hang a flag, but I was allowed to hang student art. So, students were able to create rainbow posters to correlate with every unit."

We love when compliance and resistance can work together. Go on!

> "And I am perhaps only now realizing that the conversations we had while they were making the posters were more important than what went on the walls."

And that's the rub when it comes to Pride flags in classrooms: they don't have to be big, expensive, or even "flags" at all. Students have a sense of intention and authenticity, and it's our job to work through our fear to meet them there with what we have to offer.

Books and Libraries

Now that we're through the warm-up round, let's see if we can get a little braver.

LGBTQ+ books have been having a bit of a "moment" lately, but we can't say that we're advocates for reading and literacy while anxiously Matrix-dodging an avenue for allyship. The book-banning crowd has big feelings about queer literature, usually settling on the "age-inappropriate" line when reaching for reasoning, but that argument doesn't hold true when we push back on it even a little.

I still grit my teeth remembering a junior bridesmaid at a wedding I attended years ago. Right around 11 or 12 years old, she had steadfastly refused to wear the bright pink cupcake of a dress her mother picked out for her, instead choosing a suit that matched the row of groomsmen on the other side of the aisle. Her mother sighed, telling another guest that her child was "going through a kind of tomboy phase right now." The guest shrugged and suggested that it might not be a phase and that she could also be the mother of an LGBTQ+ or gender creative kid, to which the mom responded that she "didn't want to assume anything like that" about her child, as she was "just too young."

So, to recap, this mother was fine assuming that her child was "going through a phase" but was unwilling to entertain the idea of parenting a potentially queer 12-year-old.

My hard line is: if there is a comparable straight or cisgender title, I don't want to hear a single word about the "appropriateness" of an LGBTQ+ book. It is not any more "adult" to be gay than it is to be straight. It is not any more "appropriate" for children to know about cisgender people than transgender people. *Our existence does not need a content warning.*

To be perfectly blunt about it, the banning of books, especially queer books, is a classic move in the fascist playbook. It's often a first step in the wider restriction of the kind of information and representation that helps young people learn about themselves as they start to clear a path away from shame and self-hatred. Books are how we connect with one another, they're how we communicate across time and space, and they're how we introspect and explore.

If you're looking to start or grow a collection of queer books in your own classroom, here are some good places to start:

Elementary (K–5):

Téo's Tutu by Maryann Jacob Macias

Born Ready: The True Story of a Boy Named Penelope by Jodie Patterson

Julián Is a Mermaid by Jessica Love

Kapaemahu by Dean Hamer

My Rainbow by DeShanna Neal and Trinity Neal

I Am Billie Jean King by Brad Meltzer

Middle (6–8):

To Night Owl from Dogfish by Holly Goldberg Sloan and Meg Wolitzer

The Misadventures of the Family Fletcher by Dana Alison Levy

This Is Our Rainbow: 16 Stories of Her, Him, Them, and Us compiled and edited by Katherine Locke and Nicole Melleby

Lily and Dunkin by Donna Gephart

Crushing It by Erin Becker

Too Bright to See by Kyle Lukoff

High School (9–12):

Answers in the Pages by David Levithan

The Black Flamingo by Dean Atta

All Out: The No-Longer-Secret Stories of Queer Teens throughout the Ages by various authors

We Deserve Monuments by Jas Hammonds

Last Night at the Telegraph Club by Malinda Lo

A Million Quiet Revolutions by Robin Gow

Comics/Graphic Novels

Remember: comic books are books! Just because some students engage with the written word with more interest and enthusiasm with pictorial accompaniment, it doesn't mean we have free reign to hassle them for it. Graphic novels have just as much merit as traditional literature, and it's worth including them in your collection for students.

Lumberjanes by Shannon Watters, Grace Ellis, Gus Allen, and ND Stevenson

Heartstopper by Alice Oseman

The Girl from the Sea by Molly Knox Ostertag

Gender Queer: A Memoir by Maia Kobabe

Fun Home: A Family Tragicomic by Alison Bechdel

Nonfiction

Have Pride: An Inspirational History of the LGBTQ+ Movement by Stella A. Caldwell

Out Law: What LGBT Youth Should Know about Their Legal Rights by Lisa Keen

A Queer History of the United States for Young People by Richie Chevat and Michael Bronski

Considerations for Queer Libraries

Just because we're going to be brave doesn't mean we should also be stupid. Forgive the harsh tone, but it is critical that an allied educator takes every precaution possible to protect themselves while also serving their students in whatever way they can. And with queer literature, that means *transparency*.

Before adding any queer titles to your classroom, make sure you're read up on state and local laws, as well as your school district's policies concerning teacher-curated personal reading materials. Review the book yourself, look at online reviews, and don't assume that it will work for your student population just because it's on a list. In my experience, most districts don't have clear guidance here. They might use wording like "Instructors should ensure that all books are appropriate and relevant for the student population," and we already know what a weird pitfall "age-appropriate" can be. Use your best judgment and know also that a book having queer characters or themes *at all* still means that a lot of people will have a problem with it.

In my own classroom, I made sure that my administration knew about my library and the titles within it. And at Back to School Night, I let families know that they were free to peruse any books that caught their attention, as the bookshelf was right by my front door.

It's likely, however, that you might already be in a state or a school district that has put the kibosh on queer books entirely, as they were some of the first victims of the anti-LGBTQ+ hysteria. If that's the case, consider the needs of your student population and *work backwards with the options you have*. If the need is, say:

Students need to know that they're safe here.

Or

Students need to know that these books exist.

You don't need books in your classroom to do that. Can you have pictures of books? Of authors? QR codes to digital books? Lists of books? A poster you make yourself that says "Find yourself in a book?" with the letters each colored in rainbow order?

Just like you would with a physical library, it's always worth double-checking policies to make sure you aren't putting yourself in the hot seat, but you aren't always as shackled as you think you are.

What Else Can I Do?

The physical environment of your classroom can be a welcoming and safe place for your LGBTQ+ students outside of rainbow flags and gay books, so don't think that you're trapped outside of allyship if those gestures aren't in the cards for you. Curating any kind of accessible, thoughtful, and comfortable space for your students that makes them feel especially thought of or regarded is going to go a long way in establishing trust with your most vulnerable populations and will encourage them to find value in showing up to school every day.

Here are a couple of suggestions:

- **A Menstruation Station:** If you're teaching middle or upper grades, chances are good that half of your students will spend about a week every month in relative discomfort. Getting your period at school has got to rank in the top 10 least pleasant experiences of a young person's life, and there's an extra helping of shame that comes with trying to figure out how to handle it discreetly. I always kept a basket of pads and tampons of various sizes in with other available school necessities like sticky notes and highlighters on a shelf near the back of my classroom. The key here is to store them away from the attention of the class while still making it clear early on where they are. And, as always, don't assume that you know who in your classroom might need them.

- **A Coffee Bar:** This one might sound silly, but I still think it was one of the better moves I ever made in the organization of my own classroom. Early in my career, I set up a $20 Coffee Maker on a pair of empty desks and made prepping the morning coffee part of my daily routine. Not only did it smell incredible, but it also became part of my classroom culture. Students started to bring their own empty mugs, taught each other how to clean and refill the machine, donated dish soap and a scrub brush, and built a mug rack so they could store their cups overnight – it was a blast. This specific example might not work for your classroom, but consider the spirit beneath it. When students have a chance to feel connected to you and to each other, to feel like there's room for fun and comfort in their school day, they're much more likely to want to stick around.

So, ultimately, it doesn't *really* have to matter where you're teaching (or what absurd rules you have to follow) as you build a welcoming physical space for your students – there are countless ways to make a classroom feel like a home. The largest barriers, the ones that most of us will struggle against the hardest, are usually our own. There's no law or policy or budget restriction that can keep you from signaling to students that they have a place of warmth and acceptance when they're with you. The only insurmountable dead end in this journey is our own fear. And if our queer students can find a way to survive theirs, so can we.

CHAPTER TEN

Units and Lessons

Willing to Try

In the summer between tenth and eleventh grades, my life changed dramatically. My mother, a woman who battled issues with addiction and mental health for her entire life, left our family for good and walked permanently out of my life. My father remarried, and we quickly moved 30 miles north to live with his new wife and her teen daughter. That September, I started at a new high school with an unfamiliar suite of teachers. Though the whole transition – the school, the loss, the move – was disorienting, I had the most feelings about what it would mean for English class.

This was because I wasn't immediately excited about my teacher, Ms. Charlie, a blonde woman in her middle to late forties with an enthusiasm for cardigans. She was a stark departure from the teacher I'd had at my last school: an elbow-patch-on-tweed semi-retired literature professor who was only one Robert Frost poem away from standing on desks and ripping up our textbook.

I was doubly hesitant about the change because I knew, after a quick look at the syllabus, that I had *just* read the first novel we were set to study that year: *The Catcher in the Rye*. But instead of doing what I probably would have done in her position, shrugging and saying something about how valuable it could be to read the same book twice, Ms. Charlie did something unexpected. She called her daughter, Anne, who was training to become a teacher, and arranged for her to come and visit a couple of times a week. Anne would pull me out of class and take me to the library, where she and I spent more than a month reading through Orson Scott Card's *Ender's Game*.

Anne wasn't a master of pedagogy, and neither was her mother. They didn't know a lot about differentiation or content development or unit mapping or standards alignment. They never won any teaching awards (as far as I know), and they didn't create beautiful assessments or lesson plans or worksheets. I remember very little about the conversations Anne and I had, except that she always seemed a little unsure of herself.

And those six weeks completely changed the course of my life.

I was a closeted queer kid who had just lost his mother. I had been uprooted, and I felt powerless and small in a scary and unfamiliar life. To have an adult choose to go out of their way to *see* me, to *really see* me, and try to make my experience at school better? It was transformative. I read *Ender's Game* cover to cover, I survived one of the worst years I would ever see, and by the time I graduated, I resolved to become a teacher myself.

I know there are some people who will read this book and skip straight to this chapter specifically to find the magic lesson idea that will change everything, but that lesson does not exist. *A lesson isn't anything without the teacher who teaches it, and the beautiful liberating moment you're hoping for has very little to do with your content and everything to do with how your students feel as they're exploring it with you.*

Ultimately, you don't have to have all the answers as you're developing lessons with your queer students in mind. You just have to show them that you're willing to try.

Creativity and Connection

If we aren't laser focused on writing the perfect lesson plan, what makes a unit or a lesson more adaptable and welcoming for LGBTQ+ students?

Ideally, an allied educator creates a curricular environment that is flexible, trauma informed, and rooted in both *creativity* and *connection* wherever and whenever they can. Consider my experience with Ms. Charlie. I felt isolated and invisible when I first came to her, which is an experience we see mirrored for thousands of queer students across the country. While there is a place for explicit LGBTQ+ representation in instructional materials and we know that choosing to highlight queer experiences and voices helps tremendously with a child's development and self-worth, that is a comparatively microscopic piece of what they need to see and experience in the classroom. Ms. Charlie didn't need to pick a book written by a gay or trans author to change my life; she needed me to feel valued and empowered so that one day I could *become* a gay and trans author.

And truly, lessons do not have to be stiff and joyless to be effective.

Consider what you remember from your time as a student, particularly during the intersection of puberty and your prime cognitive development. It's likely that your social and creative memories are much stronger than your instructional academic ones. That's not because academics aren't important (this isn't a "recess every day" argument) but because that's the part of your brain that was doing the most growing at that time. Adolescents are a ton of fun to teach when we remember how wild and creative their minds become as they approach adulthood. Ultimately, good teaching asks us to meet our students where they are and to challenge them within their *zone of proximal development* (ZPD).

If you're unfamiliar with that term, a person's ZPD is essentially that sweet spot in learning between overwhelm and boredom. We want to find ways to engage students, but with our hand just barely gripping the seat of their cognitive bicycle. Let go too early, pushing a child to "figure it out" before they're ready and they'll give up (and crash into the bushes). But hold on for too long, keeping them from taking the lead when they're fully capable, and they start to believe that we don't trust them to pedal on their own. This is why we need to lean into *art* and *play*, because opportunities for creativity, discussion, and social interaction are where the most allied teaching happens.

Some teachers find themselves so afraid of losing control, or of their class appearing "easy," that they will reject this suggestion outright. When I was enrolled in an education course while I was still a student teacher, I had a particularly stern professor who swore up and down that any assignment that could be considered an "art" project had no place during class time and that they should only be offered as optional homework. She told us this the same day she also mentioned that she'd worked in the classroom for only two years before taking an assistant principal promotion. So no, I will pass on her advice.

Creativity and art are not a throwaway, "rainy days only" part of teaching, and they're not the sole domain of elective classes – they should be a central and routine part of the core curriculum and within every content area.

Ask yourself these questions before moving on:

- How often is *listening to your students* built into your lesson plan?
- How often do they listen to *each other*?
- How structured are your class discussions, and are they always (or very frequently) tied to a *grade or evaluation*?
- How often do students have *control* over what they create and what they discuss?
- How often are students *smiling, laughing,* or free to be *silly* during class time?

- What does it feel like to step back and give up some of your control to them?
- If you had to distill it to a single sentence or phrase, *what is the point of your class*?
- What do you want students to remember and retain from their time with you?
- How does your answer to the last two questions change if you have to pick something that is *not content-area knowledge*?
- How often do *you have* fun in your class?

Avoiding Pitfalls

As hard as it is to admit, there *is* such a thing as a bad idea. As you're crafting discussions and lessons that you hope will uplift and engage queer students, make sure you aren't accidentally swerving into a strategy that might do the exact opposite, like one of these:

- **"Debates" about queer rights and lives:** Popular territory for social studies and language arts classes, debates can be a great way for students to practice research and speaking skills while learning how to engage in discussions about current events. There's no problem with encouraging young adults to work through feelings about controversial topics, but this one is a no-go. Forcing a child to sit in a room while their classmates list reasons why they shouldn't be allowed to get married? Or use a public bathroom? Or exist at all? That's not educational; it's cruel.

- **"My name" icebreakers:** I have controversial feelings about icebreakers, because I am an extrovert and a talker who loves a reason to gab with strangers right out of the gate, but there is a particular brand of "getting to know you" activity that is well-meaning but potentially harmful: those that ask students to share about the meaning or history of their names. For some students, this question might be asking them to:

- Out themselves as trans, because they will either have to lie about how they received their name or reveal that it was not the name they were given at birth
- Reflect on or talk about a name that they have a painful connection with, especially if your state or school site has policies against honoring chosen names

Instead, try an option like a gallery walk, four corners debate, or world café as a first-time "get everyone talking" activity. As much as we want students to learn about each other, it can be unsafe to force it too quickly. Let deeper conversions happen naturally as they connect throughout the year – you can't speed run emotional vulnerability.

- **Lessons that are not trauma-informed:** How to be "trauma informed" in your teaching is a subject for a whole separate book, but the gist is this: people, including children, who have experienced any kind of trauma in their lives have the potential to be re-traumatized by how we interact with them and what we teach. This is where the concept of "trigger warnings" came from, or the idea that we should warn captive audiences when we are about to talk about potentially sensitive subjects. There are a lot of ways to ensure that we aren't re-traumatizing our most vulnerable students, but these are some great places to start:
    - Never assume that we know which of our students are queer or which of them have experienced trauma.
    - Make a routine of asking yourself *when and how often am I asking my students to engage with depressing or traumatic subject matter?*

If you're building a lesson, discussing an event, or introducing a queer figure from history, are you generally focusing only on the parts of queer existence that are rooted in pain and suffering? Our lives are vast, complex, joyful, and strong, even if our history has been challenging. Our students will internalize the past as a vision for their future. If they are confronted only with despair, that's what they will carry with them.

Running an Effective Discussion

Don't let the potential for pitfalls scare you away from leading discussions with your students! The opportunity for young adults to test their ideas and practice listening and connecting with one another is critical not only for their individual growth as communicators but as a tool to break down the echo chambers they're already starting to build as young people in the digital age. Social media has the tremendous ability to bridge gaps of distance and to introduce us to the world outside of our neighborhoods, but because every one of these platforms – Instagram, TikTok, YouTube, whatever three new ones will exist before I finish writing this chapter – are ultimately money-making and advertising tools, they have every motivation to trap us within perspectives in which we already agree. While (some) adults can notice and try diversifying what they're consuming, it's much harder for kids. What 15-year-old who is just beginning to develop his own values stands a chance against the algorithm?

It's for this reason that modeling effective discussion strategies is good teaching, *and* it's allyship. It belongs in every single content area.

My favorite discussion model for classrooms is an adjustment to the classic *Socratic Seminar*. While you don't have to arrange desks into concentric circles, award points for participation (in fact, I suggest you don't), or discourage hand raising, here are the elements that are worth keeping:

- Begin with at least one interesting question, without students coming in with prepared written responses.
- Stay out of it as much as you can, and let students take the lead.

- Lean into uncomfortable silence and encourage students not to jump into another question right away.
- Dedicate plenty of time, if not a whole class period, to allow the conversation to evolve.
- Let students get off track, tell personal stories, and make connections to what's happening in their own school or community.
- Remember that some students participate best when they are listening and reflecting, and they may not process quickly enough to jump in right away (or at all).
- For longer discussions where students have access to technology, think about adding in "research breaks" to add context and fact checking. This is a great chance to teach some additional skills around reputable sources of information online.
- End the discussion with quiet reflective writing time, and ask students to think through where they began, what they heard from each other, and where they are now.

Even potentially silly topics and starting questions can evolve into deep and meaningful conversations when they're handled well. In one of my eleventh grade English classes, a student brought the question "Are the *Veggie Tales* racist?" to the class. If you aren't familiar, *Veggie Tales* is a children's cartoon where vegetables act out biblical stories and parables, and it's popular even outside of Christian circles. The question caused a bit of laughter and hubbub at first, but it settled into a fascinating reflection on the ways in which media influences our view of the world, especially when we're very young. Students reasoned that even if it's unintentional, when cartoons give exaggerated foreign accents to villain characters, they might develop the subconscious belief that people who are different from them are untrustworthy. One of my quietest eleventh graders raised her hand near the end of class to offer a story of her own. She and her family are Persian, she said, and she grew up embarrassed of her mother's accent. One day, when the two of them were in the mall together, she blew up at her mom and told her to shut up right as a group of her friends passed. Though she apologized after, she said that her relationship with her mother had never really recovered. The question that got us there was silly, but I will always remember the moment of absolute silence that followed her story.

When you dive into sensitive subjects and conversations with your class, just as important as core communication skills is the concept of *boundaries*. A good boundary is less about what you expect of other people and more about knowing and understanding yourself and your limits. Most young adults don't have the tools to know right away when they're dysregulated by challenging subjects or conversations, so building in moments to pause and check in with them will help as they figure it out for themselves. What they need is (generally) not to remove themselves completely, but just a minute long break to breathe and collect their thoughts.

More than just taking breaks and teaching breathing exercises, modeling the process of recognizing your own emotional limit will make it much easier for your students to understand theirs. You are a person, not a machine, and students often make comments that aren't especially conscious of that. What do you need to do to stay regulated in those moments? Do you need to pause the conversation? Take a step back? Get a drink or a snack? Stand in the sun for a moment? Do what you can to get what you need without abandoning yourself, and it will stick with them.

Bridging the Confidence Gap

When we do choose to engage in lessons or discussions that directly acknowledge the existence of LGBTQ+ people, it's okay to recognize that many educators will feel a degree of hesitation, and even fear. Schools have always been battlegrounds for conversations about identity and equity, even if the hateful rhetoric has been slowly escalating over the last decade. As you work to address where that hesitation is coming from, either internally or with other members of your staff, remember first that your primary directive is to keep yourself and your students physically and emotionally safe. You can't advocate for anyone if you get wrapped up in nonsense, so be as thoughtful as you can about when to push back and when to save your energy for a different fight.

There is a place for justifying some fear, especially as it relates to compliance with state and local laws, but a lot of it stems from an internal lack of confidence. And while neither of these issues are especially easy to address, we can try.

Remember the research I was conducting on my own campus, where I was polling staff throughout the year about LGBTQ+ student experiences and classroom support? Near the end of my data collection period, I asked 69 of our teachers to tell me what their own biggest roadblocks were: *what concerns did they have about trying out a lesson or using a strategy that could benefit their queer students?*

For the most hesitant teachers, responses looked something like this:

> "During this political climate, I am concerned with the recent attack from a political side suggesting teachers are sending their liberal agendas to our children and blaming us. I support the LGBTQ+ community 100%, but I also fear retaliation and I need my job."

One of the teachers I worked with directly, who overcame his fear of retaliation to try a lesson about the Stonewall Riots, expressed similar concerns. Though he was anxious, he decided that it was worth trying at least once, to struggle through his trepidation for the sake of the queer students in his class whom he knew were struggling with issues of campus bullying. When I asked him afterward if his worries had manifested, he admitted that he hadn't received any complaints and that his anxieties were "justified but not acceptable." Later, he wrote to me:

> "Homophobia exists, and it does feel like it could potentially invite conflict, but it's our responsibility as teachers to ensure that school is safe for everyone and that intolerance isn't allowed to fester. It is unacceptable for teachers to shy away from conflict because of our personal duties to our students."

Staff Survey Responses

Figure 10.1 shows the survey results.

- Gender-inclusive language when I address my students (for example, "ladies and gentlemen" or "guys" replaced with "students" or "everybody"): **42%**

- I ask about student pronouns privately as a part of a getting-to-know-you student survey or activity: **17.4%**

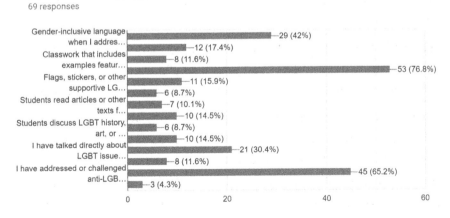

FIGURE 10.1 Survey results

- Classwork that includes examples featuring LGBTQ+ students (for example, word problems or vocabulary sentences with same-sex couples or people who use "they/them" pronouns): **11.6%**
- Signs or posters in the room promoting it as a "Safe Zone": **76.8%**
- Flags, stickers, or other supportive LGBTQ-related signs in the classroom: **15.9%**
- Students complete projects or assignments in class related to LGBTQ+ people or issues: **8.7%**
- Students read articles or other texts featuring LGBTQ+ people or issues: **10.1%**
- Students learn about LGBTQ+ figures in the history of my content area: **14.5%**
- Students discuss LGBTQ+ history, art, or current events: **8.7%**
- There are books with LGBTQ+ authors or featuring LGBTQ+ characters available in my classroom library: **14.5%**
- I have talked directly about LGBTQ+ issues or other related subjects in class: **30.4%**
- I have talked directly about the Queer Student Alliance (QSA) on campus: **11.6%**
- I have addressed or challenged anti-LGBTQ+ disrespectful behavior in class (for example, "That's so gay"): **65.2%**
- I have not implemented any of these things in my classroom: **4.3%**

But fear isn't the only reason why a teacher might be on the struggle bus when they're deciding whether to include LGBTQ+ topics in a unit or lesson. Teachers who had reservations about trying new inclusive classroom strategies had a variety of reasons, but the most common were: "a lack of training and/or knowledge" (33.3%) and "a lack of resources" (44.4%). These barriers were similarly reported by School

Mental Health Professionals in GLSEN's 2019 national survey of school counselors, social workers, and psychologists, with 40% citing a lack of training and 31% citing a lack of material resources as the primary barriers to their LGBTQ-related efforts.[1]

This makes a lot of sense. Teachers of all content areas have wildly different questions and needs. How should a French teacher address a nonbinary student, for example, when the language itself is inherently binary? How should a science teacher broach the subject of the complexity of sex and gender during a unit on chromosomes? How should a health teacher or a history teacher begin to teach a sometimes-mandated inclusive curriculum when they feel unprepared? We can't just say "be more inclusive, make these students feel represented and welcome" without offering concrete starting points and the resources to do so. And while direct peer-to-peer training and support is the ideal solution, buying a book called *Teach Like an Ally* is also a pretty good start.

Starting Points (by Subject)

While I would love for the next 40 pages to be dedicated solely to comprehensive and completed lesson plans broken down by subject, that's a touch unrealistic. Whenever we prescribe canned curriculum to teachers, it has the potential to discount our own individual classroom needs and our creativity. Think of these suggestions as starting points, as generative launch pads that will ideally spark units and lessons that will continue to evolve as you use them. The goal is to make the overwhelming task of creating a lesson a little more accessible, manageable, and easy to return to when you need some help. I hope also that this reference list also serves as a reminder that queer lives, contributions, and history are not subject-specific.

English Language Arts

- Parts of speech and the politicization of pronouns
- The design and messaging of LGBTQ+ protest buttons/pins
- Censorship and the Hays Code
- Does it matter? Analyzing if authors/characters from history were LGBTQ+ (for example, Emily Dickinson, Nick from *The Great Gatsby*, Mercutio from *Romeo and Juliet*)
- Oscar Wilde
- Truman Capote
- James Baldwin
- Audre Lorde

Project idea: The poems of the Greek lyricist Sappho were largely destroyed by the church after the fourth century, so only fragments of her more than 10,000 lines remain. What can we learn about her from just her fragments?

"Sweet mother, I cannot weave –

slender Aphrodite has overcome me

with longing for a girl."

"You may forget but

let me tell you

this: someone in

some future time

will think of us"

Ask students to write their own poems or stories about themselves, and then rip them up together. Have their peers select fragments, transcribe what they can see, and write about what they think they can learn about the original authors.

History/Social Studies
- Paragraph 175, the Pink Triangle, and the Holocaust
- The 1969 Stonewall Riot
- Christopher Street Liberation Day
- Intersectionality and the Civil Rights Movement
- Bayard Rustin
- Marsha P. Johnson and Sylvia Rivera
- Harvey Milk
- Kathy Kozachenko

Project idea: After concentration camps were liberated at the end of World War II, none of the Allied countries or new German states would recognize the men who wore the pink triangle as victims of the Nazis, and they collectively chose not to repeal Paragraph 175. Most gay men were moved from the liberated camps to other prisons to continue their sentences. When else in history have the "good guys" gotten it wrong? What do we lose when we see history as "black and white"?

World Language
- *Discussion*: why do we think some languages assign gender to nouns?
- "Elle" as a proposed gender-neutral pronoun in Spanish
- *El Tri Gay* and the International Gay and Lesbian Football Association
- The *Haute autorité de lutte contre les discriminations et pour l'égalité* (French Equal Opportunities and Anti-Discrimination Commission)
- Frida Kahlo
- Gloria Evangelina Anzaldúa
- Gabriel Attal

Project idea: As ideas about identity and language have shifted, so have the terms we use to describe our national, ethnic, and racial identities. Historically, someone with shared culture or origin from Cuba, Mexico, Puerto Rico, or South or Central America might use the word *Latino* or *Latina* to describe themselves, though two new iterations are gaining popularity: *Latinx* and *Latine*. Research why these terms are becoming popular, and compare the arguments for using either, or neither, of them.

If you have students who are part of this community, consider adding an option for them to explore which terms they like to use to describe themselves.

Science

- Medical advancements and the development of AZT during the AIDS crisis
- Reproductive and courtship diversity in nature
- Chromosomal variation in humans
- The differences and similarities between *sex* and *gender*
- Hypothetical examples and case studies using LGBTQ+ identities
- Sally Ride
- Sara Jo Baker
- Ben Barres
- Audrey Tang
- Alan Hart
- Joan Roughgarden

Project idea: As we grow up, we're sometimes taught that the world exists in a "binary" and that biology, nature, and science is simple and easy to define. What have you learned that shows how complex the natural world really is?

Math

- *Spectra*, the professional association of LGBTQ+ mathematicians
- Hypothetical examples and word problems using LGBTQ+ identities
- Alan Turing
- Sophie Wilson
- Robert MacPherson and Mark Goresky

Project idea: Have students create a survey to distribute to peers in another class and use the data to help with lessons related to statistics or other mathematical concepts. As they are constructing their surveys, discuss which demographic questions they will ask, and why. For each question, walk through and discuss how students will ask, and what purpose the information might serve. If they want to ask about gender, talk through what an accurate capturing of that data could look like. Should they include nonbinary options? Intersex? Other trans identities? What are the benefits and consequences of asking or not asking, and how will that be reflected in the quality of their data?

Visual and Performing Arts

- The history and influence of the New York "ballroom" scene
- "Untitled (Portrait of Ross in L.A.)," 1991
- *Angels in America* (1991)
- *Rent* (1994)
- *Moonlight* (2016)
- *Love, Simon* (2018)
- *The Umbrella Academy* (2024)
- Keith Haring
- Nan Goldin

- John Waters and Divine
- Andy Warhol
- Jean-Michel Basquiat
- KD Lang
- David Bowie
- Elton John

Project idea: The AIDS quilt (also called the NAMES Project) is the largest piece of community folk art in the world, conceived and constructed as a memorial to those who died during the AIDS crisis of the 1980s and 1990s, as many of them were not given funerals. The quilt was displayed on the National Mall in Washington, DC, in 1992, with more than 21,000 handmade panels.

Work with your class to come up with an issue or cause that you'd like to construct a quilt for – cleaning up the ocean, the COVID pandemic, the importance of the arts in education, etc. – and make them individually. Put your quilt together and display it for the school!

Health and Physical Education

- Overview of social and political determinants of health
- Sex education acknowledging LGBTQ+ individuals and experiences
- Mental health lessons acknowledging bullying, harassments, and LGBTQ+ individuals and experiences
- The national and international response to the AIDS crisis
- Glenn Burke
- Martina Navratilova
- Billie Jean King
- Adam Rippon
- Orlando Cruz

- Chris Mosier
- Caster Semenya

Project idea: People within marginalized communities often see higher rates of substance abuse and experience worse health outcomes. Create a poster or social media messaging campaign highlighting one of these disparities (without blaming the community for experiencing them!).

More Research Topics

- The Gay Liberation Front of 1969
- The history and color symbology of the Pride flag
- Marriage equality and *Obergefell v. Hodges* (2015)
- LGBTQ+ privacy laws and *Lawrence v. Texas* (2003)
- *Masterpiece Cakeshop v. Colorado Civil Rights Commission* (2018)
- Princess Diana and the AIDS crisis
- Contemporary LGBTQ+ political representatives
- Don't Ask, Don't Tell (1994)
- Matthew Shepherd and "The Laramie Project" (2000)
- Global LGBTQ+ issues: pick a country outside of your own and dive into what the challenges, trends, and statistics are for the queer communities there

Is It Worth It?

So, for all the trouble so many of us have experienced when we try, is it ultimately worth it? Does all this work for representation within our curriculum have any sort of measurable outcome for our kids?

Yeah, it really does.

On my campus, the teacher who worked with me closest on curricular inclusion, the one who was the most anxious about what the consequences might be? He saw, in just one classroom over five weeks, a shift from 14.71% to 0% of students answering "strongly disagree" to the statement "LGBTQ+ students face a harder time during the school day, either academically or socially." The number of students answering "disagree" to that same question dropped from 50% to 40.63%. Most students seemed to have shifted to "somewhat agree," with numbers jumping from 29.41% to 46.88%. We can move the needle, and it doesn't take much. We can help students see each other, and empathize with their experiences, if we take the time to try.

I asked that same teacher at the end of the school year if he had any regrets or if anything from the experience surprised him. There are no regrets, he told me. "Students just want to be listened to," he said, "and it's okay for them to know that you're still learning."

Notes from the Queer Teacher Survival Guide

Signs of Burnout

Burnout can sneak up on you when you live a life in hypervigilance. The following may be signs that it may be coming for you soon:

- You try to open the lock on your own front door with your classroom keys.
- You fantasize about a "mild to moderate" car accident during your morning commute.
- You stay late every night and haven't cooked for yourself in weeks.
- You've been declining invites to activities you used to enjoy because you are just *too tired* on weekends.
- You're exhausted every evening but still have trouble getting to sleep.
- You feel like you're working all the time, but you're still behind on grading.

(Continued)

> Remember, you can't pour from an empty cup. You can't give what you don't have. *Your job is important, but not more important than taking care of yourself.* That might look like a bubble bath and an herbal tea to start, but it also means reevaluating where you are putting your energy and what is taking the most from you. You might think there's no room to cut, but there absolutely is. You do not need to write up feedback for every assignment, you do not need to volunteer to take tickets at the football game, and if your work email is bouncing to your phone, shut that down right now. You have worth outside of what you do for a living. Treat and value yourself the way you want your students to emulate, because they will.

Note

1. Greytak, E., Kosciw, J., & Kull, R. (2016). From Teasing to Torment: School Climate Revisited. GLSEN.

PART IV

Beyond the Classroom

CHAPTER ELEVEN

Communicating with Families

A Letter to the Mother Who Called Me a Groomer

I am, from the deepest recesses of my heart, so truly sorry.

Not for who I am or who your child is, but for the feelings of loneliness, confusion, and resentment that have made a home in your life. Because honestly, I can't imagine a job harder than being a parent. Teaching is challenging, but when that last bell rings, I say goodbye to my students and go home to a different life. At the end of the year, I pass them along to a new set of teachers and cross my fingers hoping that they will carry something from my class along with them. But really, there's no way to know for sure. My investment, I hope, is a meaningful one, but it is still brief.

But you – you once held your child in your arms before they could speak and imagined a life for them. You manifested a world that was kind and secure and loving, and you played out how they would live in that world. You picked a name, you painted a room, you chose baby clothes, and you watched them night after night just to be sure they were breathing. You taught them to roll over and crawl and stand and walk. When they started school, you read to them every night and helped them trace the letters of their name. You watched them grow out of their shoes too quickly, you introduced them to the music you like, you picked them up early from sleepovers when they got homesick. There was a time when you knew your child better than any other single person in the world, including them.

I can't even begin to imagine how disorienting it must be, no matter how much we all know it's coming, to watch that child grow into a person. Puberty comes lightning fast and, with it, an avalanche of brain development. Neural pathways are forged, along with a host of new connections between neurons, and suddenly, that brain is in the body of a whole teenager, not a child. I know it happens to all of them, because I've been teaching high school for my entire adult life. Suddenly, the kid who once was struggling with a rolling backpack twice his size is 6 feet tall and raising his hand in the middle of class to ask "if time really exists." Students who have obediently followed their parents to Sunday church service every week since they could walk are now dodging their moms' texts, chatting at lunch, and chatting together about the paradox of omnipotence. And a star athlete who is less than a year away from a full-ride scholarship to his father's dream school is pacing in the hallway after school, rehearsing how to tell him that he doesn't want to play football anymore.

*As terrifying as it is, that change in them isn't against nature – it **is** nature. It is not only normal, but developmentally necessary, for children to forge their own identities.*

And maybe you knew that. It's possible that you saw this moment coming, but you thought it would be different. You hoped that your child's departure from your worldview would manifest as something more manageable. Something, anything, but this. You thought you raised them differently. In fact, you swear you did. You can't believe for a single moment that this kind of change came out of nowhere, or that the child you held in your arms was actually someone else all along. This has to be something forced on them, something they didn't choose. They were tricked. They were influenced. This isn't them.

And I know believing that is easier. Because the alternative is that you missed something. If what we say is true – that we were born this way – then a piece of your child has been invisible to you for their whole life. It was there in your arms, it was there when you watched them sleep, it was there when you read to them – it was there right from the start, and you didn't see it.

And sitting in that is painful.

Here, there is a grief that can't be ignored.

But instead of facing it, it is simpler to push that grief down and replace it with rage. There's nowhere to direct grief, there is nothing to do but hold it. But rage – rage is a weapon. It's a weapon begging to be used. That's when you found me.

And so, as I said before, I am sorry. I am sorry that I can't absorb your grief. I am sorry also that taking on your rage won't help you either. The truth is that no parent has ever strengthened their relationship with their child by hurting someone else. There is no one to yell at, no complaint to file, no school board meeting to attend, no bill to pass, no president to elect, that will change who your child is and always was. Seeing me might have helped them envision a path away from shame, but there's nothing I could have done, just as there's nothing you could have done, to change the essential truth of their identity.

You might be able to convince your child to hide again, to retreat into themselves, to push down the knowing that burns under their skin, but you can't reshape their heart. You can't mold the person you want out of the person who is.

And, truly, wouldn't loving them be easier?

Because it's not too late. You could start right now. There is still time to turn this ship around and rebuild trust with the person you once promised to love unconditionally. You might think it's your love that's guiding you in this moment, but that's not what this is. Fear, rejection, anger, resentment, disgust – these are feelings that don't have a home within love.

I won't anticipate that you will ever see me differently, but I will hold on to the hope that one day, not too long from now, you come back to the child who needs you.

We Are Not Enemies

Like many millennial teachers, when I first started my time in the classroom, nothing was more terrifying to me than talking to my students' families. There was a reason I had become a high school teacher. I really liked working with kids, not adults. As a 22-year-old with no experience in the working world, I didn't know how to talk to them, and I was still struggling with the basics of successfully navigating emails and calls *at all*. The idea of picking up the phone and initiating contact with someone twice my age about how their child was disrupting class? I would have rather eaten my own arm.

Luckily, as time went on and I became more generally confident and capable, parent contact was less terrifying, and it was obvious that it was central to my job. As much as the last decade or so has been building teachers and families up as adversaries in education, we aren't. We're partners, and we need to act like it. There is no inevitable existential battle for the soul of America's children; we are on the same team, and we are working toward the same goal. Approaching parents, even the most combative and disagreeable parents, with real curiosity and compassion is the only way to close this gap of understanding and collaboration.

But man do they make it hard sometimes.

What do we do, say, to find common ground with our students' families in a time of the "parents' rights" movement? This movement may *seem* to empower parents to make decisions on behalf of their children but has acted as a tool to disempower children and young adults. It also paints educators and child development experts as nefarious interlopers who are looking to indoctrinate vulnerable young people. Where do you go from there? How do you talk to someone who believes to their core that you are a predator and that you have no expertise or insight to offer in the education of their child?

Ultimately, these beliefs are rooted in fear, and there is no argument that can reason someone out of this kind of fear. There are powers much bigger than you or your students or their families that know how effective fear can be as a tool for control. There is no magic word or excellently reasoned argument that will snap someone back to a reality that you no longer share. The compassion to be found here is that *none of this has anything to do with you*. What parents who have fully bought into this worldview are afraid of is losing a connection with and understanding of their child. And while we can't change the course of their thinking, understanding where it comes from can help us tremendously. I have four tips for productively navigating these kinds of parent conversations:

- Ask questions.
- Find common goals.
- Don't be your only witness.
- Know when to walk away.

Ask Questions

When we are acting from a place of defensiveness, we can't hear arguments that challenge us, no matter how expertly crafted they are. Research, evidence, and logic need not apply; we are living squarely in the world of feelings, and that's where we need to meet them. If you are dedicated to salvaging a relationship with a parent or guardian who is parroting offensive talking points and erecting an emotional wall between the two of you, the best course of action is the pivot from trying to make your point and instead focus on curiosity around theirs. This means real curiosity, not affected or condescending curiosity. Access the part of you who really and genuinely wants to understand them. This might look like any of these:

- "Where did you first hear that, do you think?"
- "What makes you think that might be happening?"
- "Why does that scare you?"
- "Is that something you've been seeing? Where?"
- "What about this concerns you?"
- "Have you seen evidence of that? Where?"

Tone here is critical. These questions aren't accusations, they're a doorway into shared understanding. By asking questions and really listening all the way through the answers (without interrupting, correcting, or redirecting), it becomes possible not only to help them break down the wall between you but for you to get a much clearer picture of the fear. There's a reason "question asking" is one of the top de-escalation techniques from law enforcement to social work: it works.

Find Common Goals

Ideally, communities, families, and educators work together to plan and implement a vision for a child's education, because we all have a shared stake in it. For the most part, parents don't have children with the intention of hurting or neglecting them. Similarly, most teachers don't get into teaching with the hope that one day they will be able to ruin a kid's life. Believing in both parties' good intentions feels simple, but it can be the most insurmountable barrier. A good starting point if you feel communications going south is to engage in some level-setting between you. What is your most basic common goal? If you can, start by establishing that together and use it as your baseline that you can return to if you feel the conversation veering off course. This might look like the following:

- We all want this student to feel more confident in class.
- We all want this student to get to school every day and graduate on time.
- We all want this student to ask for help when they are feeling lost.
- We all want this student to find their love for reading again.

And while this is a good focusing strategy for parent, it's also a helpful tool for you. When you find yourself pulled to argue or push when a moment becomes heated, returning to that pre-established common ground can keep you from completely losing your cool.

Don't Be Your Only Witness

If you notice that a line of communication may be getting out of hand, pump the brakes sooner rather than later. We all want to feel in control of a situation and that we are capable enough to handle being put in a tough spot, but you may be doing yourself some significant future harm.

This applies mostly to calls and conferences with families, but feel free to consider it in similar situations with colleagues and administrators. If you start to get that pit-of-your-stomach feeling, that's your cue. Find a reason to close the conversation, and don't worry about how tactful you are. Way too many teachers find themselves stuck in uncomfortable or even abusive situations because they're worried about appearing rude. Be rude, it's fine. My go-to was always:

> "It feels like we can't be productive together right now. We'll try again later. Thank you."

It's not a question, and it's not a suggestion. This conversation is over.

If you engage with them again, don't do it alone. The new boundary is that communication is either written or supervised. Email is often the best option because it creates a paper trail of actions and responses, and it eliminates the need for immediate processing and response. If necessary, have someone read what you've written before you send it. For more contentious communications, I always CC'd one or two of my administrators.

In person, do the same. If you must meet face-to-face, do so only with advance notice and with an administrator present. Take notes if you can and email a meeting summary to everyone as a follow-up. It's much harder to argue against a reality to which you are not the only witness.

Know When to Walk Away

Ultimately, you are a teacher, not a therapist. If none of your strategies works and you find yourself on the receiving end of verbal and emotional abuse, walk away. You are not a punching bag, and there is nothing in the description of your job that entitles families to using you as one. You have the right to safety at work, and holding compassion for someone is different from allowing yourself to be repeatedly hurt by them. You are worth more.

If you're at the end of your rope and can no longer productively speak with a family, say something to your administrators. If you can, write up what you have attempted so far, along with as much detail about your interactions as possible. It is reasonable for you to request that all communication from here goes through your principal or vice principal, or in more extreme cases, the potential removal of that student from your class. If everyone is entitled to a productive and peaceful learning environment, you are part of that "everyone."

If your administration is slow or unwilling to act, contact your school district and find their universal complaint procedure. What you are encountering at this point may be a hostile work environment, and there will be protocols for handling it from here.

Considerations for Queer Families

In conversations about "parents' rights" or families' involvement in school life or curriculum, we almost always forget that queer families exist.

Well before the Obergefell decision in 2015,[i] same-sex or otherwise queer partnerships were raising children and establishing lives and households across the country. Some families adopt or foster, some choose to have children through a surrogate or IVF, some are raising the children of other family members, and more still might have begun their families in heterosexual partnerships but have since pivoted to different family structures. Remember also that a person doesn't have to be in an obvious same-sex partnership to be queer. One or more parents may be bi or pansexual, asexual, nonbinary, or trans – and you would never know.

The point here is this: if you've been teaching for even a single year, you have likely taught a child who comes from a queer home, and the

---

[i] The landmark Supreme Court case in the United States that guaranteed same-sex couples the constitutional right to marriage.

comfort of that student and their family matters just as much as any other. When putting together an environment and materials for your class, keep them in mind too. Here are three reflective questions:

- What can families see in your physical environment?
- What does your paperwork assume?
- Do students see their family structure at school?

- **What can families see in your physical environment?** "Safe Space" signs, rainbow flags, and supportive posters aren't just for your students – they can do a lot of heavy lifting for any queer families who may visit your campus. I remember one of my very first Back to School Nights, when a pair of men knocked on my door about 10 minutes before we were set to start. They had seen the rainbow flag in my window and wanted to let me know that they were nervous about visiting the school for the first time, but my flag made them feel just a little bit better. It was my first time accessing enough bravery to keep the flag up during a parent event (the year before I'd taken it down, anticipating backlash), and it affirmed for me just how important visibility really was – for everyone.
- **What does your paperwork assume?** Especially at the start of the school year, we send home stacks of forms, charts, and other paperwork that ask our students to review with their families. Review the wording (and the assumptions baked within) before sending it out again. Does it assume that a child has both a mother and a father? That they have two parents? That they're being raised by their parents at all?
- **Do students see their family structure at school?** When we hear talk about what is "appropriate" representation for queer identities within our curriculum, there's almost always an argument about the age threshold. But there are hundreds of thousands of children whose first interaction with queer adults starts the moment they are

born, with no adverse effects in their development. What is damaging, however, is when a child raised in a loving family realizes that their teachers and classmates don't see it that way. A lack of representation in our curriculum doesn't just hurt potentially LGBTQ+ students but also the students who are learning that some people see their family as age inappropriate.

Frequent Parent Questions and Concerns

While you can't be expected to be the ultimate expert on LGBTQ+ life, culture, and identity, some families will still see you that way. And while we can always direct parents and guardians to our recommended resources,[ii] preparing for some of their most common questions and concerns can go a long way in the forging of a connected and trusting relationship. While some families might see your relationship as adversarial, most of them do not, and you will likely be one of their first resources for better understanding their child.

It's true also that some of *you* are this parent. You are looking for help, for answers, and for understanding in a time when it can be hard to sort through the noise to find anything compassionate and useful.

The entire content of this book could be filled with nothing but the questions I have fielded from families over the last 10 to 15 years, but I have done my best to narrow them down to just the ones that are both the most common, and the toughest to Google. I hope they help.

"If my child is LGBTQ+, what can I do to make sure they know it will be okay if they come out?"

I've talked a lot with young people who grew up with families who weren't necessarily unsupportive, but they struggled talking with them about their identity anyway. Each time, these teens couldn't point to a specific moment that made them feel clearly wary, but the unease

---

[ii] My favorite books for parents are listed at the end of this chapter.

had settled there regardless. Generally, it wasn't the presence of bigotry that they sensed, but the absence of a clear sign that everything would be okay if they were to come out. Because of heteronormativity, we tend to think that every child we interact with is going to grow into a cisgender and heterosexual adult, which is statistically unlikely. Because of this, unless parents are already close with other queer family members or friends, their children don't have a good picture of how their parents might react to an LGBTQ+ epiphany. While some families choose to say straight up "If you ever realize that you like girls/boys, that will be alright and I will still love you," it can be hard to cover all your bases. You just never know what your own kid's journey will look like.

The best course of action is twofold: first, reject heteronormativity now if you can. Meaning, don't assume that your child will be straight until proven otherwise. Try to skip mentioning imagined future spouses or asking if their new friend of the "opposite sex" is a romantic interest. Let them speak for themselves and be open to change without judgment. Second, try to include queer art, film, television, and history in your life at home. If you have queer friends, don't beat around the bush about their identities. The more our lives are seen, accepted, and normalized in your household, the less likely it will be that they experience anxiety about it later. And if your child isn't queer, they're set up well for living in a world where other people are.

[About their transgender child]: "I feel like I'm mourning the loss of my son/daughter."

This is the most common feeling expressed by the parents of trans children, even from those who are the most expressive and enthusiastic LGBTQ+ allies. Truly, it is shocking and disorienting to learn something about your kid that you never expected, and there's a host of mourning processes that have to happen from here. Suddenly families are learning how to completely change the way they speak about someone they've known their whole lives, whose appearance, voice, and mannerisms may shift as they continue to learn more about themselves. As hard as this process is, it will be harder for the child, no matter their age. For this reason, I always urge struggling parents to talk through their mourning experience with literally anyone on Earth but their kid. Even though they will be the ones who know the most about who they are and what they are experiencing, it is unfair and unhelpful to ask them to guide their family through the emotional process of accepting them. Being trans is hard enough; it is not the job of a transitioning person to therapize their loved ones through it.

There are some trans people who do see their transition as a kind of "death" and don't mind using that kind of language to describe what's happening to them. There are also a ton of us who are very much put off by being referred to as someone who needs to be "mourned." It's always helpful to mirror the words and phrases we use to talk about our experience rather than to guess how we'd like to talk about it.

"I think my kid might be queer or trans. How can I tell?"

You can't! Not until they tell you, anyway. While we might be tempted to play through a kind of LGBTQ+ scavenger hunt when we suspect a child may be part of this community, it usually means dipping into stereotypes and gendered expectations that will only prolong and confuse the self-discovery process that we're all entitled to. Though most queer adults can look back and point to interests and signs that informed who we are now, there's very little good that can come from projecting our guesses onto kids if they don't take the lead. There's no harm in encouraging children to learn about themselves, having access to representation from LGBTQ+ adults, and curating an allied household (refer to the first question in this series for tips for that), but parenting shows us all the time how little control we have over who our children will become. Instead of worrying about it, give them space to figure it out on their own, and engineer a climate of trust and security between you so there's no question later about where, when, or how they might bring it up.

"My kid is trans. When I talk about my child in the past, I don't know what name or pronouns to use or how to talk about their life during their transition. Any tips?"

This is a common pitfall for families, friends, and allies, and it sounds like it would be more complicated than it really is. Usually, you'll hear a well-intentioned but misinformed family member say something like:

> "Oh yes, our daughter is trans. Back when she was a boy, his name was Jeff. He's a girl now, though, so we call him Jane."

In the switch from present to past tense, the pronouns get confused and jumbled as the speaker tries to figure out how to talk about someone who has moved through the world in different genders. To them, keeping "she" throughout might not make sense, because they're discussing a time when she wasn't using "she" yet. But from their child's perspective, they have likely been "she" the whole time. There was no time when "she was a boy," because she was not a boy, she was a pre-transition transgender girl. Though trans people all have different relationships to their pre-transition lives, we usually prefer not to be misgendered (or deadnamed) by the people who talk about us, even when they are discussing our past. I have also become fond of the phrase "before I understood myself as trans" rather than "before I was trans," and I recommend it to anyone who is looking for a place to start. So, the sentence now becomes:

> "Oh yes, our daughter is trans. She started to understand herself as trans in high school, and we love Jane very much."

"I'm worried that my child is going to have a harder life and will become traumatized if they are LGBTQ+. How do I prevent that?"

We do not currently live in a time and place that allows for the raising of untraumatized queer (and especially trans) people. If trauma is any experience that puts stress on our bodies outside of what is typical, it is unavoidable for anyone who will live through distressing and atypical experiences. And for queer people, especially trans people, that's all of us. The best and most protective families in the world can't shield us from a world that is still going through the growing pains of LGBTQ+ acceptance. The good news is that experiencing trauma doesn't mean we have to experience pain and rejection inside of our own homes. Though some families might want to reject the realities of a queer child because they fear for what that child will experience later, that denial won't save them. Consistently, we see that the one thing that most guarantees a queer child's resilience and success as they face trauma throughout their life is a close and loving relationship with some kind of family. We can't do everything for our children, but we can absolutely give them a soft place to land when the world is harsh and cruel.

Resources and Recommendations

In my time working with the families of queer children, there is often a moment where I remind them that they could learn absolutely everything about their kid's identity and still not get closer to knowing them. *Knowledge is power, but curiosity is connection.* Nothing will ever serve a parent better than developing a solid foundation of trust with their child and in approaching the process of learning about them as an exciting and unique adventure. Knowing everything about being trans is completely different than knowing everything about your unique kid.

That said, it doesn't hurt to be prepared, and there are some questions a teenager isn't well equipped to answer. The following are some of my favorite titles for families, and because parenting a queer child is complicated from top to bottom (like most parenting, I hear), not all of them are specific to LGBTQ+ life and identity:

LGBTQ+ Basics:

The A-Z of Gender and Sexuality (From Ace to Ze) by Morgan Lev Edward Holleb

The Pride Guide: A Guide to Sexual and Social Health for LGBTQ Youth by Jo Langford

This is a Book for Parents of Gay Kids: A Question & Answer Guide to Everyday Life by Dan Owens-Reid and Kristin Russo

Unconditional: A Guide to Loving and Supporting Your LGBTQ Child by Telaina Eriksen

For Learning Together:

Gender Identity Workbook for Teens: Practical Exercises to Navigate Your Exploration, Support Your Journey, and Celebrate Who You Are by Andrew Maxwell Triska

Trans+: Love, Sex, Romance, and Being You by Kathryn Gonzales and Karen Rayne

Wonderfully and Purposely Made: I Am Enough: A Journal All About Me by Cheryl B. Evans

The Trans Self-Care Workbook by Theo Nicole Lorenz

Parenting Companions:

Parenting Beyond Power: How to Use Connection and Collaboration to Transform Your Family – and the World by Jen Lumanlan

Permission to Feel: Unlocking the Power of Emotions to Help Our Kids, Ourselves, and Our Society Thrive by Marc Brackett

The Parenting Map: Step-by-step Solutions to Consciously Create the Ultimate Parent-Child Relationship by Dr. Shefali

For Trauma Work:

No Bad Parts: Healing Trauma & Restoring Wholeness with the Internal Family Systems Model by Richard C. Schwartz

We All Have Parts: An Illustrated Guide to Healing Trauma with Internal Family Systems by Colleen West

CHAPTER TWELVE

Make Your Principal Read This Chapter

Are You in the Arena Too?

In 1910, President Theodore Roosevelt delivered a speech in Paris, where he said:

> "The credit belongs to the man who is actually in the arena, whose face is marred by dust and sweat and blood; who strives valiantly; who errs, who comes short again and again, because there is no effort without error and shortcoming; but who does actually strive to do the deeds; who knows great enthusiasms, the great devotions; who spends himself in a worthy cause; who at the best knows in the end the triumph of high achievement, and who at the worst, if he fails, at least fails while daring greatly, so that his place shall never be with those cold and timid souls who neither know victory nor defeat."

It's one of those speeches that sticks with you, especially when you find yourself on the pointy end of failure and criticism, because it's not an entirely comfortable place to be. Nelson Mandela gave this speech to the captain of the South African rugby team before they defeated New Zealand. LeBron James has "Man in the Arena" scribbled on the sole of his sneakers. And we all like to think of ourselves as this person – the one on the front lines of justice and purpose, who "spends himself in a worthy cause." Most people, I think, hope that they are putting in hours for the good fight, whatever their version of that fight is.

But not all of us test that belief often enough, and this is because choosing to reflect in earnest means to be vulnerable; it means letting go of our most protective and defensive nature and leaving ourselves exposed. There is a discomfort in finding out that your course might need correcting or that you've missed a chance for courage when it was most needed. I've been there a few times over the last decade, and I don't love it.

So, I'm going to ask you to embrace that discomfort for a moment.

Because teachers and administrators, despite dedicating their lives and careers to the same cause, don't always find themselves on the same team, and I didn't always know why.

But when I was 21 years old – a brand-new baby teacher – I sat in on a high school biology class. The teacher I observed was a 30-year veteran who was still using those transparent plastic pages on a table-mounted projector, and he spent the day lecturing about the parts of the inner ear while he ate peaches out of a can with a plastic fork. He was near retirement and in his "just try me" era, and his students seemed absolutely enamored with him. At lunch, his principal came by to chat for a bit, and the moment he left, this teacher turned to me and said, "One day you will have a choice: getting in with the teachers' union or becoming an admin. Don't do admin. And remember, no principal is really your friend."

I heard something like that from every veteran educator with whom I ever taught, and I believed it without any hesitation until I started working through my master's degree in Education Administration. Suddenly, all my professors were principals and superintendents. I was studying how school budgets worked, where our state money came from, and what was asked of the people who spent the school day up in the front office – who they had to answer to and who they had to please. I learned two critical lessons in that program:

- Whatever my principal was making, it wasn't enough.
- I never, ever wanted to be one myself.

But even with this new appreciation, my feelings of general antagonism remained. I knew that the demands of the job were bonkers, but so were mine. We were both being asked to accomplish something that felt impossible, and there was still a wall between us. Something was missing.

This brings us back to the arena.

I knew I was in it. The fight lasted years, but I was there. I was showing up over and over again, and every once in a while, I would look over my shoulder. When the fight was going well, my admin and my district were behind me. When the crowd was cheering and the horizon seemed open and clear, they were there. But when the applause stopped? When the crowd turned against me? When it seemed like I might not make it to the final bell? They were gone.

And I knew why.

School districts are risk averse. Change, even solid, data-supported, peer-reviewed, historically precedented change is scary when it is unpopular. That, by definition, is what innovation is. Systems don't innovate themselves; they chase change when it looks like it's inevitable. Institutions like school districts are capable of innovation, but they are usually less willing to put themselves on the front lines if it looks like they'll also have to face pushback.

But that's what will always be waiting for us down in the arena. When we push and try and "come short again and again," there is no escaping the criticism and discomfort that comes with it. And it is worthwhile. It's worth trying our best for our kids and for ourselves, even when we know it's going to make our lives harder first.

So, if you're a principal, a vice principal, manager, trustee, superintendent – anyone at all who spends the school day in an office and not in the trenches of a classroom – ask yourself:

Are you afraid to be out in front?

Are you in the arena with us?

We're on the same team if you want to be, and it's the only way we'll ever see anything change together.

Leading a Proactive vs. Reactive Campus

At the start of the last week of the year, right on the very edge of summer vacation, there was trouble brewing at a high school on the other side of my county.

A science teacher, having wrapped up her final exams and finding herself firmly in the "reruns of Bill Nye" part of the summer countdown, was deciding how she was going to handle talking to her students about a big change.

This was because she was trans, but her students didn't know that yet. For her entire career she had come to school in a suit and tie and gone by "Mr. Whatshisname," but she knew that things would be much different by September. This was because she had finally decided to start hormone therapy and had elected for a gender-affirming surgery that was now only a few weeks away. Though she knew it was the right choice for her, she was agonizing over how to talk to her students about it. It didn't feel fair to disappear as one person and then pop back into existence as another on the first day of school. And what if one of them saw her at the grocery store in August? She lived close to campus – it was bound to happen. The best-case scenario would be to clue them in now, give them the summer to process, and return in the fall. So she decided to talk to her principal about it.

To him, she made her case:

> Ideally, she would like to talk to each of her classes individually on the very last day of school, after she had finished up all curriculum

and published everyone's final grades. In the same way a teacher might announce a pregnancy or an engagement, she wanted her students to know that there was a big and imminent change in her life. She wasn't going to entertain personal follow-up questions from students but was willing to have a counselor in the room with her, if her principal thought that might be necessary.

Her principal came back a day later with his answer:

She was welcome to tell her students about her transition, but because the conversation was of an "adult" nature, she would have to draft, print, and send home 200 parent permission forms first. Any student whose parent didn't consent to the conversation would have to be excused from class.

She was gutted.

Her principal had just, in one sentence, made her feel the most dehumanized and unwelcome that she'd ever felt in her time as a teacher. The message was clear: the support of her administrators was conditional, and it was the official policy of the school that her existence was not suited for children. Her principal was not concerned about her safety, her well-being, or her long and spotless record as an educator.

His one concern was this: *what will the parents think?*

Was it even legal to ask her to do that? Was there any kind of precedent? Had any other administrator ever asked a teacher to do something like that?

It didn't matter. She wouldn't be coming back.

The school year ended, she said goodbye to students who would never see her again, and she handed in her resignation.

Years later, when I was going through my own circus around my transition while I was teaching, I thought about her a lot. How could both of our stories have turned out differently? In theory, trans people are protected from employment discrimination under the law, but neither she nor I made it very far. It's because prejudice is very rarely overt, and it's mostly the result of poor planning on the part of the people who are supposed to be looking out for us.

As of January 2025, the US Equal Employment Opportunity Commission has issued the following statement: "...the agency is returning to its mission of protecting women from sexual harassment and sex-based discrimination in the workplace by rolling back the Biden administration's gender identity agenda." President Trump's Executive Order 14168 ("Defending Women From Gender Ideology Extremism and Restoring Biological Truth to the Federal Government") removed all mention of protections for trans and nonbinary Americans.

As an administrator, especially in times like these, you never want to see yourself forced into a corner. And this is why it's so important to build a *proactive* campus and not a *reactive* one.

A *reactive* campus is one where this teacher's principal had never considered what it would mean to employ a transgender teacher. He had no plan, nowhere to go for advice, and because it was so close to the end of the year, he didn't take the time to work through his options to come up with a solution. He let his fear of retaliation overcome his judgment as a leader.

A *proactive* campus is one that puts in the work to maintain a safe and connected culture for both students and staff, and a lot of the anxieties that come with being forced to be reactive can be avoided completely when that work is taken seriously. This means that a proactive administrator:

- Is consistently visible and available, not only to families and students, but to teachers and staff
- Works to develop and maintain the trust of their teachers throughout the year
- Visits and sits in classrooms routinely, and not just for teacher evaluations
- Is transparent and inclusive about campus decision-making
- Is honest and reflective about the current culture of the campus

And to that last point: too many campus leaders respond to disappointing and disheartening campus incidents of bigotry with the same platitude:

"This isn't who we are."

But if it's happening on your campus, especially if it happens all the time, it *is* who you are. A campus isn't its own living thing; it's a collective of individual people who act and make choices on their own. It's the response of the adults in charge that corrects the course from there. If you have an intention to provide a "safe and inclusive culture for all" and that ultimately includes tolerating bigotry and bullying, bigots and bullies are the only people who are safe and included.

So where do you go from there?

Examine your school's missions and values and test them against both the policies and the lived realities of everyone on campus. Take, for example, your social media policy, specifically the policy for members of your staff. Ask yourself:

- Is this policy actually supporting your teachers, or is it just protecting you and the school district?
- What guidelines would go the furthest for teacher well-being without limiting their right to express themselves and connect to community support networks?

Example of a proactive social media policy:
Do not film, photograph, or record students without the express written consent of both the student and their parent or guardian. General media releases signed at the start of the school year are relevant only for official school activities such as sporting events and theater performances, for publication solely on school channels such as our official website and Instagram.

The worst *reactive* social media policy is to have no policy at all. Usually, this will mean scrambling when there's any kind of incident, which is bad news for you, the district, and any teacher or staff member involved. "Soft rules," or rules that are unwritten and/or enforced sporadically, are a great way to erode teacher trust. *"But X teacher can, why can't I?"* is not only annoying, but it also often edges right up against discrimination in the wrong set of circumstances.

Reactive: "Nothing has happened yet, but we need you to take this down."

Proactive: "We think this might get some community pushback. Here are our options. You haven't broken any rules, you aren't in trouble, and we want to work with you to keep you safe."

Follow this process with as many school policies, traditions, and activities as you can. Where are the gaps? Where has a lack of reflection, time, or pressure kept your school from taking a good look at the sustainability of your culture?

Special Consideration: Club Rush

Does your school have a yearly extracurricular club recruitment or fundraising event? This was always where our queer student group saw an uptick in harassment. For some schools this year, that harassment has escalated to violence. What is the experience of the equivalent group on your campus? If you haven't thought about it, what's your plan?

And if your school has been lucky enough to escape national attention for now, don't count on it for long. With the proliferation of short-form video content and the increased hostility toward public education, the window of safety and anonymity is narrowing. Instead of fighting to squish inside the ever-shrinking status quo, start planning. When the arena calls for you, will you be prepared?

Queer Staff Protection and Management

If you read the story at the start of the last section and thought "That won't ever happen here; I don't have any transgender teachers," chances are very good that you're super-duper wrong. You might not have any trans teachers who feel safe enough to come out (either in their personal lives or just at school), but you've definitely employed at least one. We are, at minimum, 1% of the population. If the history of your school has seen 101 teachers, one of them was probably trans. And remember, at least 7.6% of the general population is LGBTQ+. For Gen Z, the next generation of teachers? That number is closer to 22.3%.

If you're having a hard time orienting yourself around how challenging this job really is for queer, and especially trans, teachers, I want to try an empathy exercise.

Imagine you are a trans teacher on the first day of school. *How will you handle introducing yourself to your students?*

Remember:

- You will have to do this six times.
- You have a choice between lying about who you are or extreme emotional vulnerability.
- How might honesty compromise your safety? Your mental and emotional stamina? The ability to do your job?
- How will lying affect you personally? What will you be giving up?
- How will you handle meeting parents at Back to School Night?
- How will you tell your colleagues? Your principal?

To be a queer teacher means to live in a state of hypervigilance, constantly oscillating between how you see yourself and how others perceive you. Black orator and thought leader W.E.B DeBois called this experience "double consciousness." For him, double consciousness meant feeling disembodied in white spaces, where he knew he was seen as an unwelcome threat. For his own survival, he could never fully relax in order to maintain the comfort of white people around him. This concept is now in common usage within a host of historically marginalized communities, and whenever those identities stack on one another within a single person, that vigilance is felt exponentially.

So how can an administrator help to relieve some of that pressure? Not just for their queer staff, but for anyone in their employ who is living through a similar experience?

Here are some starting suggestions:

- Rethink your view of "professional" attire for teachers, especially as it relates to clothing expectations by gender.
- If you're relegating denim or other comfortable clothing to Fridays (or, God forbid, asking teachers to pay for the privilege to be comfortable), stop.
- Match new teachers with a mentor teacher, with the option (on a strictly volunteer basis) for matching with someone of a same or similar identity. It's not problematic if it's teacher-led.
- Invest in ongoing professional development, even when it isn't mandated.

Remember, professional development, especially anti-bias training, isn't just for the benefit of your students. You have members of your staff who are likely sitting in the wings, waiting to see if it's safe enough to bring all of themselves to work. It's draining and dehumanizing to know that your colleagues might push you away if they only knew who you were. As an administrator, your attitude is the marker for how the rest of your staff should behave. When you do spring for training, what is your visible reaction to it? How frequently is it available? How often do you evaluate the program you use?

The world needs queer teachers, and we will only survive in American classrooms as long as there is someone left to stand up for us. As the sticker on my laptop has said for years:

Queer Teachers Are Living Proof of Queer Futures[i]

Unless we're ready for the end of that future for everyone, we're in this together.

---

[i] Sticker by Coyotesnout.

CHAPTER THIRTEEN

School Board Meetings 101

If you want to make any kind of substantial community change within education in your lifetime, you will probably have to attend at least one school board meeting. To know why, it's helpful to have a basic grasp of what a school board is, why they exist, and why they are your best bet for effecting shifts within your public school district. Essentially, public schools are a public service, which means they are accountable to the people who live in your community. Though how effective this system is in practice varies from county to county, here is the hierarchy most of them use for decision-making:

- **Teachers:**
  Make decisions about how to interpret and teach curriculum, how to interpret school policy for classroom behavior management, and how to score and assign student grades.

- **Principals and school administrators:**
  Make decisions about how to hire teachers, how to interpret district policies into school policies, how to allocate and spend some school site funds, how to organize the school day, and how to settle smaller disputes between members of the staff, families, and students.

- **School district officials (human resources, assistant superintendents, fiscal services, other department heads):**
  Make decisions about how to allocate and spend district funds, how to hire and fire support staff, how to organize the school year calendar, and, if necessary, how to facilitate some disputes between school staff, families, and administrators.

- **Superintendents:**
  Your boss's boss's boss: this is the head honcho within most school districts. They will make decisions about high-level hiring and firing, which educational or curricular initiatives will be selected and prioritized, and the overall "vision" of a school district.

- **The school board:**
  The superintendent might be the figurehead of district leadership, but the school board has arguably the most power out of anyone. Composed of (usually) three to five members, these are seats that are voted on by your community. There are no prerequisites to election: a board member doesn't need to have worked in a school, taught in a school, had children who ever attended school – nothing. The board not only makes all hiring and firing decisions for the position of the superintendent but often has the final say in the dismissal of any school employee and in the expulsion of any student, and they hold the supreme power of the district purse strings. If you want something funded, prioritized, addressed, or eliminated, it's going to be through them.

  Luckily, they have a boss too: you.

  Because the seats on a school board are elected by the community in which they serve, they have a reason to listen to you. Every four years, you have a chance to kick them to the curb for a fresh face, and they would rather avoid this. Though some school board members are not paid, the larger the district, the better chance there is that they are getting a solid payday from their position – and with good reason! An effective and engaged school board can transform a district, so we have a lot of skin in the game, and so do they.

So, let's get you ready to raise some hell.

Why We Hate Robert's Rules

If you've never been to a school board meeting, you can still probably guess how they run. Like most governing bodies in this country, from small town city councils up to grand congressional hearings, they use a system of engagement called *Robert's Rules of Order*.

Also called *parliamentary procedure*, Robert's Rules were first developed in 1876 by US Army officer Henry Martyn Robert for a reasonable purpose: to maintain some degree of control in the chaotic environment of debate within government. There are now 12 published revisions of the original guidebook, and the count of the most recent one rounds out at a healthy 816 pages, which is just about the same length as Frank Herbert's science fiction epic *Dune*.

Though there are thousands of smaller guidelines nestled within the larger ones, all with their own processes and special considerations, the general operating procedure most school boards will follow during a public meeting is as follows:

1. The board president (voted on by the other members at the beginning of the term) calls the meeting to order, meaning that they can begin dealing with official business.

2. Someone draws attention to the "minutes," which are available to the public and detail the happenings of the last meeting. The board votes to approve them, meaning there are no challenges or changes to the content. They will then do this for the agenda, which is the agreed-on list of tasks, debates, and votes that are set to happen at this meeting.

3. Trustees (another name for board members) run through announcements and reports in an agreed upon order, and any special committees or guests do the same.
4. The board moves in order through the business of the agenda, with a specific procedure for how they engage with each item. Usually, one of them will make a "motion" to begin a discussion, and another one of them will "second" it to proceed.
5. For each item on the agenda, there will be a shared understanding about what they are allowed to do within the meeting time they have. Sometimes an item just exists for "discussion," and there will be no vote to take action. Sometimes an item is voted on immediately because the discussion happened last time. Sometimes a secret third thing happens because I have been attending and participating in school board meetings since Obama's first term and I still don't know how it all works.
6. Board members may also make an amendment to a motion they have already made, meaning they want to revise their wording or suggested action to be more precise. They might ask for a member of district staff to make a report or recommendation on an agenda item. They might also withdraw their motion entirely if they discover that the timing wasn't right, that they changed their mind, or that they might not have the votes they need right now.
7. Though there often isn't a time limit to school board meetings, they generally close when they've made it to the end of the agenda. The end of the meeting is signaled by the president, who will often bang a gavel for the drama of it all.

Robert's rules allow for order, but they are also exceptionally precise and convoluted to a fault. There are specific parameters for who can speak, who can act, and how they are expected to engage with one another.

I have watched seasoned board members who have served multiple terms still trip over themselves when they forget the procedural wording they're supposed to have committed to memory. I swear that 20% of every board meeting I've observed is just trustees pausing or correcting one another when they drop the ball on parliamentary procedure.

Because when you know the rules, you control the game.

It is not uncommon to watch longtime game players use their knowledge of procedure to control, embarrass, or silence newcomers. Even when we know that these rules are arbitrary and that this kind of language is just a tool, there is still a part of us that is deeply embarrassed about being out of the know. We don't like feeling othered and ignorant, especially when we are trying to communicate about something deeply important to us.

I have watched this play out repeatedly in spaces that engage Robert's Rules. A recently activated member of the community, or a newly elected representative, will attempt to speak on something that matters to them, and they are cut off before the second word:

> "That's new business. We're on special orders right now."

> "You need to wait for the president to recognize you before you speak."

> "Stop. State your name and city before proceeding with your comment."

> "We can't address that until you submit an addendum request through official channels first. We aren't going to talk about that right now."

There are a hundred unspoken rules that are treated as bureaucratic gospel in these spaces, and it can be embarrassing and demoralizing to be so quickly interrupted and dismissed. What we never address is that knowing these rules is a kind of generational wealth. The individuals who know these rules best are not the people who have the premier or most valuable opinions; they are the people who have been in these rooms the longest, who are the most powerful and familiar with bodies of government. Yes, you can take the time to learn the rules (only 816 pages to go!), but that doesn't negate the truth of how they are often used, which is often to shut down and silence dissenting voices.

Because, truthfully, who is the most likely to be new to these meetings? And who is the least likely to have experience in these spaces?

Almost always it is young people. People of color. Queer people. People who have been disenfranchised, marginalized, and historically ignored.

And that's why we hate Robert's Rules.

So, while knowing the rules helps tremendously when you play the game, that isn't what makes you worth listening to. And if anyone within these meetings tries to use them to keep you from being heard, remember that it reflects their rigid adherence to structures of power, not your own worth and competence.

It's Parks and Rec, But Nothing Is Funny

Like attempting to climb a mountain after watching *Free Solo*, successfully navigating a school board meeting for the first time is all about setting some realistic expectations.

Remember, school board meetings are open to the public, which means the public will reliably attend. There are no prerequisites or qualifications for speakers – anyone can walk into the building, sign up to speak, and be given two to three minutes of airtime in front of a hot mic. The free and democratic nature of what is usually called "public comment" can be enlightening and inspiring, but it's just as likely to be horrifying and grim.

Over the last 10-plus years of attending these meetings, I have seen the following:

- A woman use vegetable props for a discussion about sex education curriculum. To punctuate her points regarding the inappropriate nature of any kind of sex ed, she pointed both a condom-clad carrot and cucumber at both the board and the attending audience.
- A man argue against expanding cost-free school breakfasts to students living below the poverty line, because children should "learn how to provide for themselves instead of mooching off of the government like their parents."

It would be kooky and entertaining if these were screwball characters on a primetime sitcom, but they're not. Worse still, the time set aside for public comment at each board meeting (about 30 minutes a month) will be the representative sample size of public opinion that the trustees on the school board will use to measure the feelings of the larger community. Other than the constituents they choose to interact with between meetings (which they have no obligation to do), their email inbox is the only other public forum they have. And while emails are great, it's much easier to ignore them than a flesh and blood person talking directly into a microphone.

For many school boards, this means that quite a few of their decisions are down to the numbers. If a district is considering compelling students to wear puritan collars and ankle-length skirts and a trustee hears from six members of the public who are in favor of the change and only two who oppose it, that could seal the deal. It doesn't matter that the district has a student population of 40,000 – they have heard loud and clear who is willing to show up and hassle them.

Of course, not all school boards operate this way or to this degree, but many of us don't have a clear picture of just how influential our voices can truly be.

Know the Rules, Know the Game

So, you're ready for your first school board meeting!

Let's talk about some of the basics.

Where: Most school board meetings happen in person at a physical location like a school district office, with some larger districts hosting the option for digital attendance on a platform like Zoom. The room is often filled with at least a few rows of folding chairs, with the trustees sitting on an elevated platform at the front, facing the audience. School board meeting calendars will usually list the address of the next meeting.

When: Even very small school districts usually have a website, and those websites will have a menu option called something like "school board," "board," or "board of trustees." This is where you will usually find a backlog of meeting minutes from the last few years, as well as the meeting schedule for the upcoming year. This is where you should find information about the date and time of the next meeting. If you can't find it, you can always call the school district directly and ask. At my school district, meetings were almost always the third Wednesday of the month at 7 p.m.

Who: Who attends each meeting will vary depending on the agenda. At minimum, you will see the members of the board, school district staff members (such as district security, high-level administrators, IT staff, and the district superintendent). Some board meetings are practically empty of spectators, while others are packed to the door. Keep in mind that if you are attending a meeting that is highly publicized or contentious, they might limit the number of people in the room for security reasons. Get there early if you want to guarantee a spot, especially if you'd like to speak.

What: If you don't know what's on the agenda for that meeting, district staff will usually print copies and have them available to the public. If you're there for a specific agenda item, don't expect them to get to it quickly. The agenda is listed in order, so you should be able to see when it will be addressed by the board.

Though many districts will anticipate that a meeting should last only a couple of hours, that isn't always how it rolls. Often, an agenda will feature votes or action items that are time sensitive, so the meeting end time will be pushed to its limit to complete what has to be done. There have been many times where I thought we would get to bounce by 9 p.m., but I watched as my item was pushed later and later into the evening, sometimes not making it to the floor until close to midnight. So buckle in.

Before anyone talks about anything at all, there's a laundry list of symbolic and bureaucratic tasks that have to be accomplished first. Don't be surprised to be expected to stand for the pledge of allegiance, listen to some back-and-forth about the meeting agenda from last session, and watch as special guests from local schools are recognized for achievements and given awards.

Soon, however, it will be time to speak!

If you want the chance to address the board directly (and remember, that's your best shot at influencing this system at all), here are some critical considerations:

- **You will have to request to speak.**
  Yep! You usually can't just stand in line and wander up to the mic when it's time to talk. For the preservation of order (and to keep attendees from talking back and forth until 2 a.m.), anyone who wants to address the board has to fill out what is usually called a "public comment" card before the meeting begins. They should be easy to find, as they're often right by the entrance. To speak, you will have to fill out your name, the city in which you live, and the agenda item you're there to speak to. If you want to talk about something that isn't on the agenda, there will be a spot to mark that down instead.

- **Is it on the agenda?**

  Just because your topic isn't on the agenda doesn't mean the board doesn't have to hear from you; it just means that you will likely speak first. Agenda speakers will be sorted into piles so they're called at the right time. If you don't have a pile, you'll be put into "general public comment," which means you will be called up to talk before the meeting shifts to new business.

- **They won't talk to you.**

  The board has to listen, but they don't have to respond. Again, the name of the game is *time management*, so it's built into the system for them to keep their mouths shut about what you're saying. They may address it later when it's their time to talk through the agenda items, debate with one another, and ultimately vote, but they will not speak to you directly. When you write your comments out, try to avoid anything that requires a back-and-forth with trustees.

- **Put the pressure on.**

  Don't be afraid to tell the board exactly who you are and why you care. You're a parent, a teacher, a taxpayer, a voter – you *matter*. Don't apologize for taking up space or time, because this is why they're there. They campaigned for this job, and now it's time for them to do it. Remember, this is the one time they are a captive audience in front of their constituents, and their vote isn't decided until the very last moment. When you speak, tell them what it is you want!

- **Your time is not guaranteed.**

  For particularly busy meetings, it's very likely that public comment time will be limited. Anticipate this by signing up for your spot as early as you can, but know also that they might cut your time. Most board meetings allow for comments up to three minutes (there is often a digital timer at the speaker's podium to help you budget your time), but a hefty speaker schedule could compel a change to two minutes, or even down to 90 seconds.

Finally, when you are putting together your comments to the board, do at least one run-through to check your timing! The average speaker can comfortably navigate between 100 and 150 words a minute, so try not to rush. If you're big on being prepared, you can also put together a couple of different versions in anticipation of cut time.

Here's an example to get your started, which is a real speech I gave to my own school board years ago. Because I often lose my place when I'm speaking, I bold every other paragraph.

Three Minutes

Good evening. Superintendent *Name* and esteemed Trustees –

I'm a teacher and the Queer Student Alliance advisor at *Name* High school. I was also a student at *Name*, class of 2008, and I'm here tonight to talk about the $1,400 allocated in the budget for the admin LGBTQ training that took place today.

I've been working on behalf of LGBTQ students and teachers at *District* for four years – some of you remember that I helped modify the board policy on nondiscrimination to be more inclusive with gender and sexuality. So, this is some of what I know about this population, of which I am part:

They are at an increased risk for homelessness, they have a higher dropout rate, they are less likely to continue education after high school, and they are at a notoriously high risk for suicide. These are not personal flaws: they are the direct result of the level of adult understanding and support in their lives.

We, as those adults, have a responsibility to keep politics and personal beliefs out of discussions of student support. At *District* we have a commitment to serve all of our students, and we can't do that if we don't know how. That's what these trainings are for. Without these trainings at every level, we are doing a disservice to our kids and to our LGBTQ staff. No number of awareness campaigns or slogans or support buttons can do what direct in-person action can – these trainings work by reaching those who need to be reached the most with vital information and strategies that may help an administrator, teacher, or counselor relate to and help a student in crisis. When *District* prioritizes the LGBTQ community, it sends a clear message that this district cares about us.

Also, legally, we need to catch up. We are definitely out of compliance with SB48 (FAIR act), and we have a lot to learn about Seth's Law and Title IX as they relate to this community. Most teachers on my own campus are still muddy about what their responsibilities are to these kids, and I can't imagine campuses with less visible LGBTQ groups fare better.

So yes, this money is necessary, and yes, these students deserve this consideration. Ideally, that would mean the appointment of a full-time LGBTQ community liaison, but continuing to invest in trainings like these is a good start. Thank you.

Two Minutes

Good evening, Superintendent *Name* and esteemed Trustees –

I'm a teacher and the Queer Student Alliance advisor at *Name* High school. I was also a student at *Name*, class of 2008, and I'm here tonight to talk about the $1,400 allocated in the budget for the admin LGBTQ training that took place today.

I've been working on behalf of LGBTQ students and teachers at DISTRICT for four years – some of you remember that I helped modify the board policy on nondiscrimination to be more inclusive with gender and sexuality.

At *District* we have a commitment to serve all of our students, and we can't do that if we don't know how. That's what these trainings are for. Without these trainings at every level, we are doing a disservice to our kids and to our LGBTQ staff. When *District* prioritizes the LGBTQ community, it sends a clear message that this district cares about us.

Also, legally, we need to catch up. We are definitely out of compliance with SB48 (FAIR act), and we have a lot to learn about Seth's Law and Title IX as they relate to this community. Most teachers on my own campus are still muddy about what their responsibilities are to these kids, and I can't imagine campuses with less visible LGBTQ groups fare better.

So yes, this money is necessary, and yes, these students deserve this consideration. Ideally, that would mean the appointment of a full-time LGBTQ community liaison, but continuing to invest in trainings like these is a good start. Thank you.

90 Seconds

Good evening, Superintendent *Name* and esteemed Trustees –

I'm a teacher and the Queer Student Alliance advisor at *Name* High school, and I'm here tonight to talk about the $1,400 allocated in the budget for the admin LGBTQ training that took place today.

At *District* we have a commitment to serve all of our students, and we can't do that if we don't know how. That's what these trainings are for. Without these trainings at every level, we are doing a disservice to our kids and to our LGBTQ staff. When *District* prioritizes the LGBTQ community, it sends a clear message that this district cares about us.

Also, legally, we need to catch up. We are definitely out of compliance with SB48 (FAIR act), and we have a lot to learn about Seth's Law and Title IX as they relate to this community. Most teachers on my own campus are still muddy about what their responsibilities are to these kids, and I can't imagine campuses with less visible LGBTQ groups fare better.

So yes, this money is necessary, and yes, these students deserve this consideration. Thank you.

Notes from the Queer Teacher Survival Guide

When You're "In the Arena"

"If you are not in the arena getting your ass kicked on occasion, I am not interested in or open to your feedback. There are a million cheap seats in the world today filled with people who will never be brave with their own lives but will spend every ounce of energy they have hurling advice and judgment at those of us trying to dare greatly. Their only contributions are criticism, cynicism, and fearmongering. If you're criticizing from a place where you're not also putting yourself on the line, I'm not interested in your feedback." – Brené Brown

Queer teachers end up hearing a lot of advice from people who have never been "in the arena" with us, especially when we are knee deep in an exceptionally challenging situation. Remember that most of the people who are offering their point of view are doing it from a place of comfort and stability, but usually not from experience. This isn't just true for strictly cisgender and heterosexual voices either – there will always be other queer people who will try to argue that you should be quieter, smaller, and less visible in your work. Ultimately, you are the only person who gets to decide how much to risk and what fights are worth your energy and pain. When seeking advice, comfort, or counsel, just be sure to check first – is the perspective you're hearing down in the arena with you or safely tucked away up in the bleachers?

CHAPTER FOURTEEN

LGBTFAQs

Allied teaching is a long-haul game, and it's constantly evolving. There's just not time in a single book to address every corner of this work, and there is still so much to say and explore. For now, I hope this chapter can help tie up at least some of the loose ends, as it's kind of a potpourri of questions and predicaments I've faced from teachers, students, administrators, and everyone in between. Fingers crossed that you're able to find insight here that helps as you continue to grow, because we're never quite done.

Quick Tips for GSAs

The following questions are ones I see a lot from adults who work frequently with LGBTQ+ students, especially as staff advisors for GSAs. While the answers aren't only helpful for them, if you find yourself signing up to host a gaggle of queer kids in your classroom at lunch a couple of times a month, you likely won't make it out without facing at least one of these predicaments.

"*My students keep 'coming out' to me, and I never know how to react. What am I supposed to say, and why do so many of them tell us before their parents?*"

It is a privilege to be a trusted adult, and nothing makes that clearer than the moment when a student chooses to disclose something as vulnerable and scary as their own self-discovery. Knowing how to respond is tough, because you want this kid to know that you're taking them seriously without appearing too casual about it. First, if you had suspicions that they were LGBTQ+, don't tell them that. It's not as validating as you think so hear that someone else knew who you were before you did. Generally, what we're looking for when we first "come out" to someone is unambiguous enthusiasm. My favorite response is something like this:

> "Thank you for trusting me with that, and I'm so excited for you! That's amazing!"

Refrain from the need to tell them that you have a gay or trans cousin/brother/barista for now and let them have a moment of acceptance with zero conditions. You can always follow up with questions to signal that you're willing to help from here, because they might be telling you as a step toward explaining an issue with harassment at school or a struggle at home.

As for why students so often come out to their teachers before any of the other adults in their lives? For the same reason I told my dentist I was trans before I told my dad: it was scary as hell when I was first figuring out who I am, and my dentist can only disintegrate the fabric of my reality so far. A relationship with a teacher is brief, and the consequences are a lot lower than with someone closer to them, like a parent or a sibling. Teachers often serve as a "warm up" as they gather the courage to try it again.

"Romances are part of life in high school, but the students in my GSA seem to be dating and breaking up all over the place. What's up with that?"

As someone who is part of an identity group that is constantly accused of "sexualizing children," the frequency and conspicuousness of high school romantic relationships always made me *deeply* uncomfortable. There's something about seeing a student kiss his girlfriend in the hallway after confidently telling his peers that chocolate milk comes from brown cows that makes me want to scream "Please no, you are a literal child."

For queer students, relationships are complicated by the extremely shallow pool of dating options at their disposal. Combine that with the fast-tracked emotional intimacy and codependency[i] that stems from maturing as a queer person under traumatizing circumstances, and you have a recipe for quick burning "friends to soulmates to enemies" arcs multiple times a year. It makes a lot of sense when you think about how isolating it must be to be a queer teenager and how relieving and joyful it is to discover a reciprocated crush under even more typical circumstances. And while these relationships are often super adorable, they are more prone to emotional overwhelm and sometimes even abuse.

Ultimately, don't let your discomfort keep you from treating LGBTQ+ puppy love the same as you would for their straight and cisgender peers, and remember that students are entitled to a degree of privacy, especially when it comes to communicating with families. If it's against school policy for two students to be mackin' behind the bleachers and it's expected that you have to phone home to let their families know why they're being reprimanded, there's no reason to expand with details that are no one's business but theirs. As much as we want to be transparent with families, our responsibility ends after we disclose to them the strict basics of the situation. You just never know what a student might be coming home to.

---

[i] Codependency is a relationship dynamic that isn't always a romantic one but is typically characterized by one person "giving" to the other in an unequal and generally destructive pattern.

> *"The situation for LGBTQ+ people in this country just keeps getting worse, and while I want the students in the GSA to find the fire within them to step up and fight back, they only seem interested in infrequent low-key lunch meetings and not much else. How can I convince them that we need their voices now more than ever?"*

A lot of teachers who are first asked to advise their campus GSA might picture facilitating a group of fired-up young leaders champing at the bit to march in the streets and "burn down the cis-tem," and that's sometimes true, but not usually. The years where I saw the most inspired student activists were the ones where my students felt the safest. And while that might seem backwards, it's because a young person who has to worry about their physical safety doesn't have the capacity to put themselves in further danger.

The morning after the 2024 presidential election, when it became clear that this country was preparing for a second Trump administration, LGBTQ+ crisis hotlines saw a 700% jump in calls and texts from people fearing for their immediate futures in the United States.[1] So as much as we want to look to the younger generations to save us, it is irresponsible to expect children to be activists. They are, ultimately, just kids. It's unfair enough that they are living through such an unsafe and uncertain time.

This snapped into focus for me the first time a student asked to come along with me to a staff meeting to speak to his experiences as a trans person. My colleagues kept posing questions to him as if he was an expert with all the answers. After the fourth or fifth one, he threw up his hands and said, "I don't know, man. I'm just a freshman!"

Visible activism, especially activism so closely tied to your own identity, can really mess you up after you've been at it for a while. Sometimes young people accept the consequences before they have a chance to understand them, and it's hard to walk away. While we should support and uplift our students who choose to take up the fight, we should pump the brakes before we ask it of anyone else.

To make your GSA feel as physically and emotionally safe as possible, consider swapping a sign-in sheet with names for one with student ID numbers (if they're required for student groups at all), work with club leadership to plan fun low-key activities throughout the year, and limit "trauma dumping" (the practice of piling on depressing and intimate personal stories without the consent of all listeners) by building in time and space for emotional sharing in healthy ways.

Logistical Nightmares

"I'm a theater teacher, and I take my students on a handful of overnight field trips every year. For financial and safety reasons, students have to room together in groups of three to four. I have quite a few students who are gay, lesbian, bisexual, pansexual, trans...you name it. How am I supposed to put together room assignments?"

For every teacher attempting to navigate overnight field trips in this or any year, I do not envy you. I was a chaperone and co-organizer on quite a few of these, and I'm not sure we ever escaped one without *some* problem, and it was always a crisis that needed to be solved at like 3 a.m.

No matter how you choose to do the math of this, it is critical that you set clear expectations, including accompanying consequences, well before your departure date, and then follow through on them when the time comes. The teacher I always worked with on these trips was a *master* at them, because she was a textbook over-planner who had seen every possible disaster that comes from not anticipating hiccups. The key for keeping the train on the tracks is consistency. If the rule is "No one leaves their hotel room after lights out, or else you can't come on the next trip," follow through on it every single time. Because it doesn't really matter who rooms with whom if your students know what behavior is and is not tolerated. Assign three to four students a room, as you don't want any opportunity for two unsupervised students to have extended time together alone. It increases your chance of shenanigans, yes, but also of bullying, harassment, and sometimes even violence. The same is true for any adult chaperones. Unless they are the parent of one of your students, there should be zero opportunity for them to be alone with a child.

When you're deciding how you want to handle room assignments, your first stop should be checking on your district or school site policy. If there is one, stick to it, even if you disagree with it. *This isn't the time for improv.* If it isn't a particularly forward-thinking rule (many districts still have the thought that boys should room with boys and girls with girls), take the time to explain it to your students and why it's important to follow some policies closely to keep all of you safe. For more ambiguous policies, talk to students about their thoughts and comfort levels as you decide how you want to handle it. It's worth a private conversation with trans students,[ii] as your assumption about where they would feel safest might not be the correct one.

For the whole process, be up front and follow through with the *why*. Tell them that their room assignments and the policies that govern them aren't there to shame their relationships or identities but to maintain accountability for the adults who have to keep them safe.

"Every year I dread yearbook handouts and graduation name reading for my transgender students. What options do they have to ensure that they aren't deadnamed or outed to our entire campus?"

This can be a tough one depending entirely on where you live, but here's a basic breakdown of how to approach this: first, if a student has had their name legally changed, the school has an obligation to update it in their records, which shouldn't be a long process. The change will be reflected in their class schedule, any online portals, on their transcript, and ultimately on their diploma. A yearbook might be a different problem, as those are often sent to print well in advance. If a student has paperwork for an official name change in, say, April, there's likely little the school can do about how their name appears in the yearbook.

[ii] That is, trans students who are "out" to you, not students you suspect may be trans.

If the student's name is not legally changed, how it's handled is up to the school. In some places, like California, there are state protections in place that should allow them to update their name to a "preferred name" on all unofficial documentation, such as a class schedule and student ID card. Because yearbooks usually pull student names from the same system that stores the information for the ID cards, that is probably good to go, but without a legal name change, a student's transcript and diploma will likely reflect their given name. In weird gray areas like this, it's often about finding and contacting the person responsible for tracking and updating whatever system you're hoping to change. ID cards are usually the realm of the Activities office (which will have an adult staff Activities Director), the yearbook is prepared by either the Associated Student Body (ASB) or a yearbook class (which will have a staff advisor), and all the specifics around graduation will be handled by one or more designated staff members. Often, all you have to do is ask.

Also, graduation ceremonies look very planned and official, but if you've ever worked one before, you know how much everyone is just trying to make it through with the last bit of end-of-year willpower they can muster. Very rarely are student names kept on some master unchangeable list. Usually, graduates are handed a little paper card to write their name, which they will hand to a person at a microphone, who will then read it as they walk across the stage. If this is the system at your school, the name reader will read whatever you hand to them. As a teacher who has read names at graduation ceremonies before, I can tell you that this system can sometimes have some hilarious consequences.

"I'm always nervous handing my class over to a stranger, and I feel like my anxiety has gotten worse with the substitute teacher shortage. What can I do to preemptively protect my LGBTQ+ students when someone I don't know is leading my class?"

There's no realistic way to completely control what happens in your room when you aren't there, but there are some measures you can take to make it less likely that there is an "incident" with a sub while you are away. First, we are rarely fully prepared when the need for a sub arises, and anything you can do to cut down on the stress of throwing something together at the last minute will help tremendously.

I had a "sub plans template" that I saved to my Drive and always emailed it to the substitute teacher with the principal and front-office administrator cc'd. In it, I not only had a breakdown of the day's lesson (anything more complicated than a page was very rarely followed, so I tried to keep it simple), but a copy of my handwritten seating chart and a bullet-pointed list of my most important class policies. This is why it is so important not to write any sensitive information on your seating chart – if I don't know for absolute certain that my sub will be respectful of my trans and nonbinary students, I'm not going to leave any clues as to who they are. My instructions always laid out very clearly that attendance should be taken from the chart and not from the attendance office-provided roster. For the most part, my system worked well – but not always.

This is why this second tip is most important: take the time to develop a relationship of trust between you and your students. This means that you shouldn't immediately assume that notes left behind by your sub are 100% accurate. Before losing your cool with a class after reading a scathing sub note, sit with them and ask questions about how the day went, what happened during class time, and what they accomplished. If there was a credible issue, don't punish the class collectively. Modeling this calm and reasonable process will make it a lot more likely for a student to confide in you when something problematic happens on the part of the adult in the room in the future.

Annoying Questions

The difference between a question asked in "good faith" and a question asked in "bad faith" is that a bad faith question isn't hoping for an answer. Some of the most pervasive queries posed to queer people are as exhausting as they are redundant, and if I could banish them from discourse forever, I would. Sometimes answering these questions is less about the peace of mind for the person who asked, and much more for anyone else who might be listening. So here are my answers to some of the most common ones:

> "I don't want my straight kids to think I don't care about them. Aren't we alienating the rest of our students by addressing the needs of an ultra-minority group?"

The reality the asker of this question is hoping for – one where teachers only consider the needs and comfort of the majority of their students – has existed before. In fact, in the timeline of American education, it's what most of our history has looked like. Every major shift in public education has been in the attempt to widen who we serve and address who we're leaving out. And each time we try, the majority are not worse off for it. Expanding education to include women did not destroy men. Integrating public schools did not increase the suffering of white children. Building wheelchair ramps, widening doorways, and installing elevators did not harm able-bodied kids. Hiring SPED teachers and standardizing IEP access has not hurt the education of neurotypical students. Every. Single. Time.

This question is a way to excuse a lack of accountability and soothe the ego of a person who isn't interested in learning or growing. Instead of reckoning with the internal discomfort that might make someone reconsider their biases, this question allows them to instead believe that turning away from their LGBTQ+ students is okay and crowns them as an advocate for justice. Well, it doesn't. This perspective is as boring as it is bigoted, and no one is impressed.

> *"I don't like being called 'cis.' In my opinion, 'cis' is a slur."*

It's not, and you're fine.

Cisgender is a term much like *heterosexual*, *able-bodied*, or *neurotypical*, in that it is an adjective to describe a person whose identity and experiences are more common and typical than their counterparts. The reason why these words exist is because the word we used to use was just "normal," and that's rude as hell to the rest of us.

Cis is a prefix to the root word *gender*, and means "on the same side as." This means that someone who is cisgender has a gender identity that agrees with the gender they were assigned at birth. This is, as far as we know, *most people*. *Trans* means "across, beyond, or on the other side of." This means that someone who is transgender has a gender identity that diverges somehow from their gender assigned at birth. To get to the root of why there are some cisgender people who insist that *cis* is an unacceptable derogatory term, I usually ask what they would prefer for us to use to describe them instead. The answer is usually something like:

"Nothing! I'm just a woman! Just a regular, normal woman!"

Ah, there it is.

People who are uncomfortable with *cis* don't like it because they do not see trans identities as legitimate. Using *cisgender* to describe them legitimizes *transgender*. So no, *cis* is not a slur. No one is targeted, harassed, discriminated against, or otherwise disparaged for being cisgender, no one legislates against your body or your rights for being cisgender, and if your only gripe is finding yourself in the same linguistic grouping as trans people like me, that's incredibly lucky indeed.

"How could what I said be offensive? They didn't say they were offended! They didn't tell me they were upset! In fact, they were joining in!"

This line of reasoning is upsettingly common for teachers, and it's one I've had to walk adults through countless times. It might also be the only question in this section that is unfairly characterized as "annoying," because it isn't always asked overtly in bad faith. I'm annoyed by it though, so here it stays.

Because this is almost always the way it plays out after a person has made a comment, joke, or insinuation at someone's expense, especially when what they said was objectively racist, sexist, homophobic, transphobic, or some other kind of -ist or -phobic. When someone who has said something harmful doesn't immediately understand or accept it, the next step is to become defensive, often citing the lack of a reaction on the part of the targeted person as a reason why they are both innocent and blameless. But here's why that doesn't fly:

There are 1,001 reasons why a targeted person, especially a child, will not push back in a situation like this. *Marginalized people survive by playing along*. Laughing *with* the people who are actively putting us down is sometimes the only way to peacefully exist, especially when we are outnumbered. The alternative, which is to stand up for ourselves and shout down our bullies, doesn't work that often, particularly when we're faced with an insurmountable power dynamic.

And this is why we need allies in every room – because it might not be safe for us to stand up for ourselves. But when the bullies are the ones who are outnumbered, we're all better off.

Notes from the Queer Teacher Survival Guide

Your Gay Enemies

I wish it were true that all of us were in this together, but we're not. Unfortunately, in the fight for queer equity and liberation, there are quite a few of us who are ready to turn away from unity and solidarity for the furthering of their own self-interest. Beware of:

- **Ladder pullers**

    A ladder puller is the queer colleague who fought tooth and nail for a seat at the table, only to close the door shut behind them. These individuals have no interest in seeing the rest of us succeed alongside them and believe that we (collectively) achieved ideal representation the moment they (individually) started to earn respect and credibility from within a given institution. A ladder puller is identifiable primarily through the belief that they have nothing left to learn and may be heard saying "We did it! I made it in!"

(Continued)

- **Infighters and gatekeepers**

    Any community will see a degree of headbutting, especially in organized decision-making groups, but there's a line that we seem to cross way too often. Consider: is this person taking a stand from a place of love? Or is the anger within them a product of guilt and shame? Our community has made an identity out of *standing on business* and *speaking truth to power*, but cruelty is another beast entirely. Remember, many of us exist day-to-day from a place of unhealed trauma, and not everyone is ready to work through their internal blocks. A good rule to prevent your own descent into infighting and gatekeeping is this: who is harmed here? Is your life, or the lives of your queer siblings, materially affected by a lesbian who uses "he/him" pronouns? Or by a bisexual woman who wants to bring her husband with her to Pride? We have too much working against us to keep creating new problems for ourselves.

    Both points of view come from the same shared mindset: scarcity. We are worried that, when we finally find an in-group that likes and accepts us, we're only moments away from finding ourselves on the outside again. But we're not. There is enough room for all of us, and we only survive the worst of what's to come if we do it together.

Note

1. Cross, Greta, "Hotlines Experience Influx in Crisis Calls Amid 2024 Presidential Election," USA Today, November 7, 2024, `https://www.usatoday.com/story/life/health-wellness/2024/11/07/lgbtq-hotlines-crisis-center-presidential-election/76092268007/`

Acknowledgments

I spent the first decade of my adult life encouraging thousands of young people to find their voices through their writing. Even my first job in college, after some disappointing years in high school working the grocery store balloon counter, was as a writing tutor in my university's library. The first time I ever sat down with a student, the two of us puzzled through the pitfalls of transitional phrases and thesis statements, I felt a light and a warmth in the center of my body that has never faded. I have known since I was 18 that this is what I am supposed to be doing. So, as I hear all the time, I may not be in the classroom anymore, but I will always be a teacher.

That is why the first person I want to thank is my mom, Janey. She didn't carry me, deliver me, raise me, or even meet me until I was already an adult, but she has been my mother in the moments when it really mattered. A teacher who has nurtured thousands of students from kindergarten through high school, Janey still found room in her heart for me when I felt like a shadow of myself. From backpacking across Catalina Island to rushing to cover a class during a panic attack to knitting a surprise Pride beanie on the eve of my coming out, you are exactly what I mean when I say *Teach Like an Ally*. We should all hope for our children to know the love of a classroom like yours.

And to Jess, who reached out to me for a doctoral dissertation interview and was immediately suckered into six months of brainstorming and revision meetings, frantic texts at 11 p.m., and a friendship that I know will last much longer than our publication deadlines. And to Max, Sebastian, and Theo: thank you for letting me borrow your mom for a while. Don't worry, I will continue to send you routine updates as to the health and well-being of our chickens.

And to Xilo, my husband, my business partner, and my best friend: we knew each other from the first moment we met, and I am so excited to settle into the life we deserve together. I don't know what's coming for us as a country, but I am ready to face it side-by-side with you.

Finally, I don't think any book on justice and allyship should exist without an explicit and deeply felt thank-you to black women, who have been at the front of this and every fight from the very beginning. We owe so much in educational equity to women like Lucy Craft Laney and Dr. Gloria Ladson-Billings, and LGBTQ+ Pride would not be possible without visionaries like Audre Lorde, Angela Davis, Laverne Cox, Roxane Gay, and Marsha P. Johnson. Thank you for what you have done, and continue to do, even when it seems like no one is listening.

Index

A
AB 1266 (School Success and Opportunity Act) (California), 21
AIDS epidemic, 49
Allied teaching, evolution, 197
Ally pitfalls, 78
Allyship, 75–76, 137
  chance, 85–86
  intentions/attention, 67–68
Ally sticker, usage, 123
American social/civic life, scrubbing, 36
Anchor bias, 71
Antagonism, 173
Anti-bias training, 180
Anti-LGBTQ+ bills, ACLU tracking, 53
Anti-queer/anti-trans legislation/policy, 54–55
Astley, Rick, 86
Attendance procedures, 107–110
  call and response attendance procedure, problems, 109

B
Bad faith questions, 204–207
Bathrooms
  equity/access fights, 15
  passes
    degendering, 112
    extra credit points, ignoring, 112
    maintenance, 112
  policies, 110–112
"Battle of the Sexes," 16
Bigotry
  campus incidents, 177
  issue, 165
  toleration, 177
Blood pressure, attention, 25

Body traumas/fatalities, report, 57
Book banning, 6, 24
Boundaries
  conept, 139
  respect, 102–103
Breaks, usage, 139
Breathing exercises, teaching, 139
Briggs, John (Briggs Initiative defeat), 38–39
Brockway, Bruce, 38
Bryant, Anita (banana cream pie, impact), 37–38
Bullying
  prohibition, 25
  safety issues, 68
  toleration, 177
Burnout, signs, 150–151

C
California
  AB 1266 (School Success and Opportunity Act), 21
  Proposition 6, defeat, 38–39
  school site funding, daily student numbers (relationship), 107
California Healthy Kids Survey data, 55, 56f
Call and response attendance procedure, problems, 109
Campus resources, availability, 74
Cancer nonprofit job, impact, 65–66
Card, Orson Scott, 132
Carter, Jimmy, 39
Catcher in the Rye, The, 131–132
Centralized values, presence, 64
Change, scariness, 173
Chappell Roan (Kayleigh Rose Amstutz), 48

Children. *See* Queer children; Transgender children
  bargaining, 90
  LGBTQ+ life, difficulty/trauma (parental question), 167–168
  loss, parental mourning, 165–166
  name/pronoun usage, parental question, 167
  needs, clash, 90–91
  protection, scare tactics, 14
  queer/trans characteristics, parental question, 166
  sexualization, accusation, 198–199
  vulnerability, 56–57
Children's Hour, The (Hellman), 35
Civil Rights Act of 1964 (Title VII), 40
Classroom policies, 99
  attendance procedures, 107–110
  bathroom policies, 110–112
  changes, 106
  evaluation, 107–114
  safety/control issue, 105–107
Classrooms
  discussion, running, 137–139
  flags/signage, usage, 120–124
  guidelines, creation, 103
  home base, absence, 123
  language, shift, 86–89
  LGBTQ+ issues/history, 11
  physical environment, welcoming/safety, 128–129
  practices, considerations, 68–69
  rainbow-washed classrooms, 75–78
  space, checking, 117–119
  staff volunteer supervisions, 104
  starting points, 143
  systems, safety/control issue, 105–107
  teacher name, selection, 114–115
  time, loss, 109–110
Club rush, harassment, 178
Coffee bar, availability, 129
Common Core, alignment, 47
Communication skills, importance, 139
Community resources, availability, 74
Companies, Pride collections (reduction/elimination), 76
Confidence gap, bridging, 139–143
Consequences, enforcement, 104–105
Control, absence, 79–80
Conversion therapy, state ban, 58
Corporal punishment, legality, 57
COVID-19 lockdown, teaching issues, 21–22
Creativity, art (relationship), 134–135
Culture war, 12–13
Curiosity, connection (equivalence), 168
Curricular environment, creativity/connection (impact), 133–135

D
DeSantis, Ron (HB 1557), 13, 22
Diagnsis/treatment, mishandling (effect), 118
Differences, student perception/treatment, 72–73
Discomfort
  danger, contrast, 101
  embracing, 172
Discussion, running, 137–139
"Don't Ask, Don't Tell" (DADT), 12
"Don't Say Gay" (HB 1557), 13, 22–23
Double consciousness, experience, 179–180
Du Bois, W.E.B., 179–180
Dune (Herbert), 185

E
Echolalia, 83
Ender's Game (Card), 132
English Language Arts, content/project idea, 144–145
Eplee, John (social contagion statement), 51
Equal Employment Opportunity Commission (EEOC), employment discrimination, 40
Equity, goal, 120
Executive Order 14168 ("Defending Women From Gender Ideology Extremism and Restoring Biological Truth to the Federal Government"), 176
Expectations, setting, 107–114
Exposure, result, 172

F
Failure, appearance, 69
Families
  common goals, finding, 160
  communication, 155
  communication, witnesses (presence), 160–161
  queer families, 22, 162–164
  questions, asking, 159–160
Feelings
  children, accountability, 93
  facts, contrast, 49–52
Fishbowl life, 29–30
Flags
  Pride flags, prohibition, 123–124
  usage, 120–124

Florida
    "Don't Say Gay" (HB 1557), 13, 22–23
    "Parental Rights in Education" bill, 22
Free speech, place, 100–101
Front office, responsibility/role, 172–173
Frost, Robert, 131

G
Gatekeepers, 207–208
Gay enemies, 207–208
Gay, Lesbian & Straight Education Network (GLSEN) data, 49–50, 143
Gayness, question, 67–68
Gay-Straight Alliance (GSA), advice, 197–201
Gender
    centering, campus commitment, 16
    identity
        change, attempt, 58
        disorder, 8
    norms, modeling, 17
    transition, videos (creation), 5
Gender-affirming surgery, initiation, 174
Gender-neutral pronoun, usage, 87–88
Generation Z, self-identification, 48
Good faith questions, 204–207
Grace, modeling, 69–70
Great Gatsby, The (Fitzgerald), 63

H
Harassment, increase, 6
HB2 bathroom bill (North Carolina), 20–21
HB 1557 ("Don't Say Gay" bill) (Florida), 22–23
Health education, content/project idea, 148–149
Hellman, Lillian, 35
Herbert, Frank, 185
Heterosexual marriage/romance, book features, 16–17
High school romances, presence, 198–199
History studies, content/project idea, 145
Home base, absence, 123
Homosexuality
    criminalization, 34–35
    DSM mental illness designation, 7–8
Hormone therapy, initiation, 174
House Un-American Activities Committee (HUAC), rise, 36

I
Individualized education programs (IEPs)
    access, standardization, 205
    handling, 73
Infant mind, women guidance, 33

Infighters, 207–208
Institutional knowledge, 7

J
James, LeBron, 171–172
Johns Committee investigations, viciousness, 36

K
Knowledge, power (equivalence), 168

L
Ladder pullers, 207
Late-work policy, strictness, 105
"Lavender Scare," 36
LGBTQ+
    advocacy, 19
    allyship, 74
    anti-LGBTQ+ bills, ACLU tracking, 53
    books
        appropriateness, 125
        availability, 124–126
    FAQs, 197
    flags/posters, issues, 120–121
    issues, temperatures/tolerance, 20
    library, curation, 5
    lunchtime event, problems, 77–78
    population, percentage, 179
    puppy love, 199
    situation, worsening, 199–201
    teaching, history, 29
    visibility, 41–42
    youth
        anxiety/depression/suicidality (GLAAD report), 55
        surveys, 49–50
LGBTQ+ students
    accommodation, 118
    affirming/welcoming, 86–87
    campus safety, foundation, 19–20
    experience survey, 119f
    fear, 121
    respect/inclusiveness, 121
    safe/affirming environment, 47
    school days, difficulty, 119f
    signs/signals, 117
Libraries
    administration knowledge, 127–128
    LGBTQ+ books, availability, 124–126
    queer libraries, considerations, 127–128
Life
    changes, 131–132
    queer life, debates, 135

Lord of the Flies, The, 105
Love, Loretta, 23

M
Macy, Mia (gender transition), 40
Mandela, Nelson, 171
Math, content/project idea, 147
Media
    influences, 138–139
    social media, impact, 137, 177
Medical facilities, avoidance, 117–118
Menstruation station, availability, 128
Mental health, boundaries, 102–103
Milk, Harvey, 38–39
Mindset
    change, 71
    environment, 83
    establishment, 65
Moms for Liberty, 23–24, 121
Moral education, influence, 32–33
Mother, letter (example), 155–158
"My name" icebreakers, usage, 135–136

N
name/pronoun usage, 167, 205–206
National Center for Transgender Equality survey, 51–52
"No hands handshake" (student development), 85–86
Norms, responsibility (sharing), 103–104
North Carolina, HB2 bathroom bill, 20–21
Nye, Bill, 174

O
Obergefell v. Hodges, 13, 162
Office personnel, questions, 173–174
Order, maintenance, 89
Outcomes, importance, 79–80

P
Paperwork, assumptions, 163
Parents
    communication, witnesses (presence), 160–161
    complaints/protests, 6
    concerns, 164–168
    contact, 157–162
    letter, example, 155–158
    love, expression, 165
    mourning, 165–166
    questions. *See* Children.
        asking, 159–160
        types, 164–168
    rights, movements, 158

Parliamentary procedure, 185
Participation, importance, 171–172
Peer-to-peer training/support, 143
Perceptions, change, 71
Perfection, problem, 70–71
Performing arts, content/project idea, 147–148
Physical education, content/project idea, 148–149
Physical environment, 117
    families, perception, 163
    welcoming/safety, 128–129
Pitfalls, avoidance, 135–137
Positively Gay Cuban Refugee Task Force, 38
Power
    knowledge, equivalence, 168
    struggle, 89–93
Pride
    flags, prohibition, 123–124
    imagery, 75
    signage, 120
Principals
    behavior, problems/issues, 175
    role/responsibility, 183
Proactive administrator, responsibility/role, 176
Proactive campus, leading, 174–178
Proactive social media policy, example, 177–178
Professional development
    benefits, 180
    theory/strategies, impact, 63–64
Puberty, approach, 156
Public schools, LGBTQ+ equity, 11–12
Punishment, avoidance, 90

Q
Queer books, list, 125–126
Queer children
    resources/recommendations, 168–169
    soil (metaphor), examination, 53–54
Queer experience, 67
Queer families
    considerations, 162–164
    structures, acknowledgement, 22
Queer libraries, considerations, 127–128
Queer literature, book bans, 124
Queer lives, politicization, 54
Queerness
    discovery, 5
    identification, damage (assumption), 51
Queer people
    agenda, 17
    existence, trauma, 72
    visibility, 41–42

Queer rights/lives, debates, 135
Queer staff, protection/management, 179–181
Queer Student Alliance, 23–24
Queer students
    relationships, complexity, 199
    run-through, appearance, 75
    safety, 68–69
    shame, experience, 89
Queer teachers
    accusations, 34–37
    current status, 40–41
    pressure (relief), administrator
        (assistance), 180
Queer topics, highlighting (opportunities), 78
Questions, annoyances, 204–207

R
Rainbow flag, usage, 122
Rainbow washing, 75–78
    ally pitfall, 78
Ramaswamy, Vivek, 51
Rapport, establishment, 84–85
Reactive campus, leading, 174–178
Reading, Writing, and Arithmetic (three Rs),
    teaching, 32
Reagan, Ronald, 39
Representation, importance, 7
Research topics, usage, 149
Resignation, 6
Resilience, modeling, 69–70
Reward/punishment systems, shame
    origin, 89–90
Robert, Henry Martyn, 185
Robert's Rules of Order, 185–188
Role model, meaning, 31–32
Role-playing, usage, 75
Room assignments, logistics, 201–204
Roosevelt, Theodore, 171

S
Safe space
    consequences, enforcement, 104–105
    defining, 99–100
    discomfort/danger, contrast, 101
    models, 102–103
    norms, responsibility (sharing), 103–104
    rejection, 100–101
    time management, relationship, 101–102
SAFE ZONE sign, usage, 122
Same-sex dates, attendance (student
    barring), 15–16
Satanic panic, 13
"Save Our Children" campaign, 37
School board meetings, 183
    agenda, understanding, 192
    basics, 189–195
    comment time, guarantee (limitations), 192
    navigation, 188–189
    occurrence details, 190–191
    presentations, examples, 193–195
    speaking, request, 191
School boards
    decisions, numbers (impact), 189
    responsibility/role, 184
    Robert's Rules of Order
        problems, 186–188
        usage, 185–188
    seats, election, 184–185
Schoolhouse door, data, 54–55
Schools
    administrators, responsibility/role, 183
    culture/curriculum, LGBTQ+ inclusion/
        representation (arguments), 15
    districts
        officials, role/responsibility, 184
        risk aversion, 173
    identity/equity conversations, 139–140
    site funding, daily student numbers
        (relationship), 107
Schroer, Diane, 40
Science, content/project idea, 146–147
Section 504 (Rehabilitation Act of 1973),
    handling, 73
Self-discovery, timeline (absence), 71
Sexuality norms, modeling, 17
Sexual orientation and gender identity
    (SOGI+), 47–48
Sexual orientation, change (attempt), 58
Shame
    projection, 69–70
    student experience, 89
Signage, usage, 120–124
Social media
    doxing, 6
    impact, 137
    policy, 177
    proactive social media policy, example,
        177–178
Social studies, content/project idea, 145
Socratic Seminar, 137–138
Speech, offensiveness, 206–207
Spirit week, hosting, 16
Staff survey, responses, 141f–143f
Stonewall Riots, 140–141
Students. *See* Queer students; Transgender
    students
    advocacy, 5
    behavior, classification, 91
    campus resources, availability, 74

Students (*Continued*)
　check-ins, 112–114
　community resources, availability, 74
　differences, perception/treatment, 72–73
　family structure, observation, 163–164
　greeting, 84–85
　hormone therapy, understanding/
　　discussion, 174–175
　marginalization, effects, 90–91
　outcome, curriculum (impact), 149–150
　policies, impact, 106
　queerness, knowledge (assumption), 136
　rapport, establishment, 84–85
　surveys, 112–114, 118, 123
　survival, 132
　teacher
　　apologies, appearance, 71–72
　　approach, 91–93
　　control, 91
　　tension, diffusion, 92
　　transformational one-on-one, 93–95
　　trans student, deadname listing, 108
　　trips, room assignments (logistics),
　　　201–204
Suffering, sharing, 5
Superintendents, role/responsibility, 184

T

Teachers. *See* Queer teachers
　activities, 8–9
　fear, 121
　impact/power, 3–4
　inspiration, 4
　interaction, 121–122
　logistical nightmares, 201–204
　name, selection, 114–115
　problems, 30
　questions/needs, differences, 143
　questions, prohibition guidelines, 113–114
　retaliation fear, 140–141
　role/responsibility, 183
　safety, worry, 31
　self-worth, 161–162
　starting points, 143
　support team, assistance, 94
Teaching
　allied teaching, evolution, 197
　ally behavior, 91
　attraction, 3
　public profession, 29
　women's profession, expectation, 34
"They," usage (issues), 87–89
Time management, safe space
　(impact), 101–102
Tinker v. Des Moines, 14

Title IX, passing, 20
Tolerance, paradox (safe space rejection),
　100–101
Transgender children, care (affirmation),
　13–14
Transgender educators
　communication, witnesses (presence),
　　160–161
　defensiveness, 159
　enemy, family perception, 157–162
　parent beliefs (origin), fear
　　(impact), 158–159
　questions, asking, 159–160
　self-worth, 161–162
　teaching, attraction, 3
　tone, importance, 159–160
"Transgenderism," perspective, 51
Transgender Law Center, Macy case
　argument, 40–41
Transgender students
　bathroom issues, 110–112
　norms, pushback, 18
　self-harm, 110–111
Trans student, deadname listing, 108
Trauma-informed lessons, usage/
　importance, 136–137
Trevor Project, data, 49–50
Trigger warnings, concepts, 136–137

U

"Under God" phrase, addition, 36
Units/lessons, 131
US Trans Survey, 20

V

Visual arts, content/project idea, 147–148
Vulnerability, 172

W

"We All Belong," empathy/understanding
　(goal), 76–77
"Week of Caring," 76–77
Women
　lady-ness, 33
　"nurturing and moral character," 33
　sexual harassment/sex-based
　　discrimination, protection, 176
World language, content/project
　idea, 145–146

Z

Zone of proximal development
　(ZPD), 133–134